The Los

by

Janet Lynden

ISBN: 978-1-917293-93-8

Copyright © Janet Lynden

2024

All rights reserved, including the right to reproduce this book, or portions thereof in any form. No part of this text may be reproduced, transmitted, downloaded, decompiled, reverse engineered, or stored, in any form or introduced into any information storage and retrieval system, in any form or by any means, whether electronic or mechanical without the express written permission of the author.

And Therefore As A Stranger
Give It Welcome
There Are More Things
In Heaven And Earth
Than Are Dreamt Of
In Your Philosophy

Hamlet

Prologue

A Pupil's Return

'Hello Sir.'

I had been gazing at a picture on the wall momentarily lost in a world of my own.

'Mm what's that you say?'

As I turned towards the figure in the doorway I gasped when I recognized one of my old students.

'Sam?

Samuel Truman.

Well as I live and breathe.

How are you?

It's been how long now since you left?

To go to Uni wasn't it, that's right you wanted to be a doctor.'

'Fat chance of that now Sir.'

As I reached him I was shocked to see how much he had changed from a fine strapping young lad to this figure slumped against the frame of the door.

He had lost an awful lot of weight and his face was pinched with fatigue; and his eyes, once so full of life and wonder were now dull and ringed with black shadows.

His voice was still melodious however but there was a quaver to it now.

He appeared to stagger slightly so I suggested he sit down but he refused saying that he would probably never get up again.

I placed a comforting hand on his arm, I was shocked at his appearance and my heart bled for him.

'What happened to you Sam?'

Here he took a deep breath that sounded almost like a sigh.

'I was halfway through my studies when I started feeling very tired and I was having bad headaches. I put it down to overwork and took some painkillers but the headaches became unbearable so I went to see the Uni doctor who sent me straight to A&E.

To be honest I was stunned, I think I had just expected him to say that I had a virus, but to be sent to A&E really shook me up.'

I could feel his whole body shuddering under my hand now as he spoke so I gently guided him over to a chair where he sank down gratefully.

I was almost too afraid to ask, 'and what was the outcome?'

A shadow crossed his face that was once so handsome and horrifyingly his chin wobbled slightly, and it was painful to see.

'After having loads of tests and scans they told me, reluctantly, that I have a brain tumour and unfortunately, they are unable to operate as it is embedded in too deeply'.

To say I was thunderstruck was putting it mildly, I was devastated to hear such bad tidings from such a young man whose whole life was only just beginning.

'Is there absolutely nothing they can do for you, chemotherapy or something like that,' I asked.

I knew I was clutching at straws, but to be honest, mere words failed me so I just spoke the usual platitudes.

The shake of his head spoke volumes.

'Oh Sam, I am so, so sorry.'

'Not as sorry as me sir.'

'Why then, as you are so ill, have you come to see me of all people?

Surely you should be in hospital or at least taking it easy.'

'Sir, you were the one person I always felt safe with and I wanted to see you...one last time.'

Most of my students couldn't wait to see the back of me so to hear Sam utter those words touched me more than I can say.

'How about a hug lad?'

'What's that sir, I don't think I've ever experienced one.'

'Well, come here and I will show you.'

Helping him to his feet I embraced him tightly but he felt so fragile beneath my hands I was afraid I might hurt him.

I first met Sam when he arrived here as a frightened, skinny eleven year old.

Big school can be especially daunting but he seemed particularly terrified.

I later found out that his father had threatened him with a beating if he didn't do well.

At first he was timid, introverted and scared of his own shadow and at one point I was very worried about him when he came to class with scars on his arms. He was pretty adept at hiding them though pulling down his shirtsleeves whenever he saw me looking.

I had spoken to him about it but immediately he would be on the defensive saying it was nothing he couldn't handle, and he would smile reassuringly at me, but his eyes told a different story.

However, as the years went by, he proved to be a very able student and he also filled out and grew taller but the threat of his father's cruelty always hung over him like a black cloud.

One day he asked me what someone could do concerning a bully.

Very often he would sit in the empty classroom at lunchtime with me while I ate my sandwiches. I usually tried to avoid the staffroom as it was always too crowded and noisy for my liking; and sometimes I just needed some peace and quiet so I could reflect on the way my career was heading.

'Who is bullying you,' I asked even though I was very aware of the answer already.

He was quiet for a long time considering his answer.

'My father, but you know that already don't you sir.'

'Yes, I do.'

As I mused over what I should say I happened to recall what someone had once told me regarding bullies.

He had said, 'stand your ground and embrace the fear.'

And then with a twinkle in his eye he had added, 'or failing that run!'

I imparted this piece of wisdom to Sam and I later learned that he had become rather good at sprinting.

As we pulled apart I felt strangely emotional; I would have liked to have had a son but we had been blessed with three wonderfully challenging daughters that I absolutely adored.

It was the end of the week Friday night, and I was tired; I am an old man now way past retirement age, and I am slowing down.

Also, trying to educate these young adolescents who think they know it all was becoming increasingly hard.

When I first started teaching it was with a passion, I desperately wanted to enlighten these young minds, but as the years went by, I came to realise what an uphill, frustrating task I had taken on, and now, what with Sam's sad news, I felt quite bereft.

Turning away from him so he couldn't see the tears in my eyes I went back to my desk and after piling all the books together I rammed them haphazardly into my battered old briefcase.

I was going home to my wife and family and to hell with this job.

'Come on Sam, you had better be off now.'

I hated myself for being so abrupt with him but he had told me earlier that he had a hospital appointment anyway.

'Yes sir,' and he appeared crushed at my unexpected brusqueness.

And then, throwing on my jacket from the back of the chair, I was immediately propelled back to another time and to another jacket and I had to grip the back of the chair tightly as my legs turned to jelly.

'Are you alright Sir?'

Hauling himself upright Sam came over towards me consternation written all over his face.

And then, when he touched my shoulder to comfort me another vision took me back.

'Oh!'

I let out a low moan and sank down heavily onto the seat of the chair putting my head in my hands as I did so.

I was a miserable failure, all these years wasted.

I moaned again.

'What is it sir?

Should I fetch someone?'

The fear in Sam's voice brought me swiftly back to my senses.

'No, no lad.

I'm fine.

No need to worry.'

I gazed up at him dejectedly.

The worried expression on Sam's white face, his skinny frame and shaking hands brought back long ago memories that troubled me still, and then I felt ashamed frightening him like that when he was so ill himself.

Struggling to my feet I said, 'come on Sam, let's go.'

'If you're sure sir,' and his agitation was clear to see.

We walked down the stairs together arm in arm, I think we were actually holding each other up.

Out we went through the school gates and as we proceeded along the road to the corner I espied a group of my latest students huddled together there.

They gave me a disgusted look as we passed by them and the mood I was in I couldn't resist giving them a cheesy grin.

'Alright boys and girls, enjoy your weekend, see you next week.'

I felt their contempt for me now as I always did.

'Stupid ol' f.......'

'Doesn't know what e's talkin' abaht.'

I could always hear their raised voices as they pushed and jostled each other as they made their way out of the classroom.

I almost felt sorry for them, but not quite, kids could be very cruel.

I desperately wanted to get home, put my feet up, and have a glass or two of sherry, but instinctively I knew that Sam needed my company and I couldn't just abandon him.

As it was now beginning to get dark and a chill wind had blown up I suggested we have a hot drink in a cafe I often frequented.

By now Sam was ashen and starting to shake visibly so as we entered I steered him gently over to a vacant table in one corner.

When the waitress came to take our order he just sat there with his head lolling to one side on an upturned hand and to be honest I felt really quite anxious about him.

'Does your head hurt Sam?'

'Mm,' he muttered.

I ordered for both of us then, coffee for Sam and a hot chocolate for me.

'Is that ok with you,' I asked him.

He nodded and then a small smile spread across his face.

'What's so funny?'

'Nothing Sir, it's just that you always did love your hot chocolate. I remember you used to bring a thermos flask full of it and then drink it at every opportunity.'

'Yes, you're right ' I grinned back at him.

'I'm rather addicted to the stuff.'

Feeling rather like a kid again I reflected on how alone and terrified he must be feeling right now.

I had been in a very bad place myself once, not in the same way as Sam of course, but I had needed help desperately and I had received it from a rather unusual source, and my throat tightened at the memory.

Sam peered at me questioningly obviously noticing how the expression on my face had changed.

'What is it Sir?

What's troubling you?

Did you lose something or someone years ago that meant an awful lot to you and you can never talk about it as it hurts too much to remember.'

I thought ruefully that I had been the lost one, but yes, I had.

'In class sometimes,' he continued 'we would often be aware of you gazing out the window with a wistful look on your face.'

Such a young man and yet so perceptive.

Before I could utter a single word the waitress brought our order to the table and glancing shyly at Sam gave him such a sweet smile.

'Thank you miss,' I said and her dark eyes twinkled in the lamplight making my throat tighten again.

Changing the subject hurriedly I remarked to Sam, 'I think she likes the look of you,' and I beamed cheekily at him.

The poor boy blushed beetroot red.

Returning to what he had asked me my first reaction had been to say nothing but gazing at him now I thought maybe my story might help him in some way.

I took a deep breath.

'In a way you're right Sam and what I am about to tell you happened a long, long time ago when I was just a lad maybe two or three years younger than you. I must warn you though that some of it is quite harrowing.

Are you still willing to hear it?'

I was pleased to see that immediately he appeared quite animated and curious at what I was about to relate to him.

'Yes sir, I should like that very much.'

'It's a tale that many people would find hard to believe, even my dear wife doesn't know what happened to me and that is why I have kept it close to my chest for so long.'

'Tell me sir.'

As I sat back in my seat and closed my eyes I let my mind drift back over the years, and as I did so I lost all sense of time and place.

1

The Lost Soul

It was Christmas eve. Snow had fallen steadily during the night and London town lay hidden beneath a thick, white blanket that glistened in the early morning light.

Nelson, from his perch high in the sky, surveyed this scene with his one, unblinking eye and in the distance Big Ben has just chimed the hour.

It is eight o'clock, and all is well.

All, that is, save for me...

I must have appeared a pathetic figure as I sat huddled on a cold, hard bench in Trafalgar Square.

Humming tunelessly I rocked to and fro in a frantic effort to ease my troubled mind and pain-wracked body.

It is bitterly cold and the frigid air causes my eyes to water and my nose to run and I wipe the snot away with shaking fingers.

The lights on the Christmas tree in the middle of the Square twinkle and wink mischievously at me but I am in no mood to appreciate them as a gloom of despondency has settled uncomfortably upon me.

My name is Mike, and I'm sixteen years old; I am also a runaway, thief, drug-addict and...I rent my body out to anyone willing to pay for it.

My hair falls in rats' tails around my face and neck, it is full of grease and probably other unmentionables as well.

Well, what would you expect?

I have been living rough for the past two years and as long as I get my regular, 'fix' I couldn't care less about anything else.

However this morning, even though I have become accustomed to living out-of-doors now I am heartily sick of this mere existence.

Trafalgar's pigeons flap-flap constantly around me calling for food but I have none to give, and even if I had I wouldn't bother to feed the pesky feathered creatures anyway.

As I gazed dejectedly about the Square I happened to spot the small nativity scene that has called to curious children and sight-seers over the last few weeks, and out of a sudden desire to see what all the fuss was about I rose stiffly to my feet and crunched across the snow to take a look.

I gazed glassy-eyed at the humble figurines and they in turn stared blankly back; they are as cold and as lifeless as I am, I turned away not looking back, sick at heart.

The traffic is beginning to build up now and the big stores to open their doors, and tourists and last-minute shoppers weave their way around me as if I am something unclean.

Well, I suppose I am.

Perhaps I should get a little bell and ring it as I go past them; I am a person of the streets, homeless and destitute.

And I am a junkie.

I sleep in shop doorways in a cardboard box when I can find one and beg for money, not for food, but for my addiction to heroin.

I'm sixteen and the way I'm carrying on, I will be lucky to see seventeen.

Last night I was invited, by who I thought was a friend, (I hasten to add here that junkies don't really have friends) to go to a party.

Cleaning myself up the best way I could I ended up in a dingy basement flat crowded with people I didn't know.

The noise was deafening and the sounds emanating from the trio of musicians was hideous but I thought I would stick it out for a while just to escape the rapidly deteriorating weather.

Halfway through the evening this, 'friend' asked me to follow him into a room at the back, and as I thought maybe someone was peddling drugs in there, I unsuspectingly went with him.

The room was in darkness as we entered and a small shiver of alarm ran down my spine as the door swung shut behind me.

At once the room was flooded with light and I found I was surrounded.

I didn't have a prayer!

They forced me down onto a bare mattress that stank of dirt and urine and my jeans and pants were viciously torn off.

And then as I was forcibly held down, a gag was stuffed roughly into my mouth to stifle my screams and then three of them gang-raped me while the others laughed and cheered them on.

I have been in some pretty desperate situations but none compared to this.

It was ferocious and brutal.

After they'd had their fun at my expense they left me alone in the room but not before giving me a few well-aimed kicks.

Somehow shivering and shaking from shock I managed to sit up and gasping and spluttering barely able to breathe I yanked the now blood stained gag from my mouth.

With difficulty I proceeded to drag on what was left of my ripped clothing, and then as luck would have it I happened to notice something that looked suspiciously like a roll of money down by my feet; the state I was in I don't quite know why I was bothering , but if it was money, then I was going to have it.

Sure enough it was, probably drug money bound tightly with an elastic band, one of them had obviously dropped it during the scuffle, and now I had it.

Stuffing it into the pocket of my jeans I stumbled from the flat as inconspicuously as I could, as along with my clothing they had managed to destroy any shred of decency I had misguidedly been clinging to, which I might add wasn't much.

Drowning in a sea of pain and despair I was now no longer a human being, but a black empty void of nothingness.

My eyes ached with unshed tears, but crying had never helped me before and it sure as hell wouldn't help me now.

The humiliation and ugliness of it all burned deep inside me and I found that my fierce hatred of them threatened to engulf me, but I was just a kid, alone and helpless, and there was no way I could ever exact revenge.

For the rest of that interminable night I wandered aimlessly about, oblivious to the world around me until I found myself slumped on that unyielding cold bench in Trafalgar Square.

The strains of carols being sung in highly-pitched voices pierces my now pounding head and grates on my fragile nerves making me want to scream -

I don't believe in God!

If a loving God existed he wouldn't have let my father abandon me to fend for myself against the cruelties my mother's lover inflicted upon me.

I had been twelve years old, a mere child and I had no say in who my mother decided to shack up with.

No, religion is definitely not for me; it's for people who really need it like little old ladies in Sunday hats and children who still believe in the tooth fairy and Father Christmas, not for the likes of me, dirty drop-out junkie.

Even so, this morning I am sick of this sordid, nightmarish existence.

Tired of sleeping on the pavement, of always being wet; of dragging myself through the streets in all weathers craving the drug on which I rely, and the relentless search for the money to buy it with.

Also too, is the constant threat from creeps last night who rob you of the smallest amount of self-respect you may have desperately been holding on to.

Up until then I had been lucky enough to steer clear of that unspeakable torture, but now I have nothing left.

No hope at all that eventually my life could be turned around and I would be saved from the madness of this hell, so all I want to do now is die quietly somewhere.

But not here.

Not in this man-made concrete jungle where human cockroaches crawl out of every nook and cranny.

I don't want to end up on a cold mortuary slab with no name and no one to give a damn.

But where, where could I go?

Then I recalled that ever since I was a child I have always wanted to go to the seaside and had never been lucky enough to have that wish granted.

Well, it was going to be granted now.

Eventually, I decided on Lands End in Cornwall - it seemed quite appropriate really as it would also be my end.

The man who dropped that money was unwittingly going to free me.

He has given me a way out of this wretched life, this existence, that I no longer wanted or needed.

I was going to buy a train ticket, and as I have no plans to return to this awful God-forsaken place, it will be one way only.

2

Mike

Never in the whole of my life, have I ever felt as alone as I do now.

Depression cloaks me like a heavy, grey overcoat and refuses to lift and as I stand trembling on this cold, draughty platform black waves of despair threaten to overwhelm me.

I worry that the train will be delayed or cancelled even due to the bad weather but eventually the guard waved me aboard and I found a compartment with only a few passengers inside, for that fact alone I am grateful as I have no wish to be scrutinised by so-called, 'normal' people, as today I feel anything but.

Leaning my head wearily against the icy window pane in an effort to ease the incessant throbbing I listened to the last-minute slamming of doors and then with a sudden jolt the train moved off.

After a while as I sat back in my seat I looked around me at my fellow travellers.

There was a young woman opposite humming softly to the sleeping infant on her lap, an elderly man who appeared to be dozing judging by the awful noise he was making and a couple of teenagers clasping hands as if there were no tomorrow. They appeared nervous and were constantly looking about them as if afraid they were going to be caught.

I wondered vaguely what they were running from and then as I watched, the girl, seemingly satisfied they were safe, leaned her head lovingly onto the boy's shoulder, and he in turn, bent his head to gently kiss her.

A moment of jealousy surged through me, but I had decided what I was going to do and must just stick to the plan.

The last few years of my life have been a waking nightmare, and there had been no end in sight, until now.

I sighed sadly.

The express was gathering speed now and as we left the dark ugly buildings and alleyways of London behind open land stark and wintry started to replace them.

Out here as in London, snow has fallen thickly and all along the route gnarled trees stand tall and strangely dignified as if in defiance of the wintry weather, their naked branches heavily laden under a layer of glittering crystallised ice, and the hushed silence was broken only by the noise of the passing train.

Gazing again at the young woman cuddling her small child I wondered if she would make a better mother than mine had been.

As I allowed my mind to travel back over the last six years of my life a hard knot began to form in the pit of my stomach.

I had been a fairly ordinary sort of kid I suppose, that is, until my father left home one day right out of the blue.

It had been just after my tenth birthday and then I changed into an angry, unhappy being that hated the world and everybody in it, including my mother.

I don't think I realised it at the time but deep down, I think I secretly blamed her for the departure of my much-loved father, probably quite unfairly.

I never saw him again, or found out the reason for his leaving either although I suspect it was almost certainly for another woman.

He had always been a bit of a Jack-the-lad with the girls but in all my wildest dreams I never for one moment believed he'd leave my mother for one of them.

Shortly after this miserable episode my mother decided to add salt to the wounds by inviting one of her male customers to come and live with us.

Obviously she was keen on him but I don't really know if it was reciprocated.

She had been working as a barmaid, more for the company than the money as she was pretty well off in her own right.

Eddie Cross was his name, Cross by name and cross by nature, and he hated me on sight. The feeling was mutual, I couldn't stand him either and protested long and loudly until a swinging fist sent me flying.

What really hurt the most though was the fact that my mother hadn't come to my aid or even bothered to lift a finger to help me.

Life for me now would never be the same again. He would go to the pub, come back drunk as a lord, and then lay into me for no other reason than he could.

He was a sadistic bully, and unfortunately for me, whenever our paths crossed, he tortured me relentlessly.

I was taller than him and slightly built and he was short and fat with a massive beer gut, and he hated that.

He would slam me up against the living room wall with my arms in a vice-like grip behind my back and then whisper in my ear all the sordid things he wanted to do to me.

I was a young, vulnerable boy and he found great pleasure in making me gasp at some of the explicit foul mutterings he liked to frighten me with.

Eventually, in my distress, I became so scared that he would physically abuse me instead of just talking about it that I told my mother the things he had been saying.

Big mistake.

She slapped me hard across the face and told me in no uncertain terms not to make up such filthy, disgusting lies.

Unfortunately my mother told him what I had said and in a fit of pique he took his belt from around his trousers and thrashed me soundly with it until I cried out for him to stop.

In just a few months he had reduced me to a gibbering idiot who jumped at the slightest noise and shook like jelly whenever he was around.

I lost an awful lot of weight as most of the time I felt too nervous to eat so I had taken to wearing baggy clothes in an effort to conceal my skinny frame.

The crunch came one Thursday evening when my mother had gone out to her weekly bingo session.

He'd come home earlier than usual from the pub and finding her not there had rampaged around the house sending anything in his path flying.

Alas for me, this was one of my rare nights at home as I was trying to stay out of his way as much as possible.

With sweat pouring from my hands and with my heart in my mouth I curled up in one corner of my bedroom fearing the worst as I listened to the din he was making.

Momentarily everything went quiet - the hush before the storm; and then the bedroom door flew open with such force it came off its hinges and landed by my feet with a resounding crash.

His face was crimson with anger, his watery pale blue eyes bulging in his frog-like face and he reeked of stale tobacco and strong alcohol.

Stomping over to where I was crouching he picked me up bodily and literally threw me across the room where I hit the wall with a sickening thud.

I must have passed out for when I came to, he was lying on top of me. I was naked from the waist down, he had his hand clamped savagely around my mouth and nose almost suffocating me, and he was trying to force himself on me.

I can still feel the weight of him and smell his hot, smelly breath on the back of my neck.

Just in the nick of time I heard the front door slam announcing the return of my mother.

Groaning with frustration he struggled to his feet punching me in the face as he did so.

Afterwards, when I had managed to crawl to the bathroom, I threw up all over the floor, my body a mass of bruises, my head pounding.

From then on pain and fear were my constant companions and I was sure my mother knew what was going on but she just didn't care. She ignored me most of the time anyway, I was a nuisance and I am quite certain she would have been very glad to see the back of me.

I left in the early hours of a cold February morning vowing never to return. With not a penny to my name and only the clothes I stood up in I walked the streets aimlessly desperately needing someone to hold me and tell me everything would be alright, but there was no one.

Eventually, wretched and alone, I made my way hitch-hiking to London where I assumed all runaways made for.

I felt like I was a nonentity, and that is how I thought people saw me so I decided that I would find a quiet hole somewhere and just keep myself to myself.

Between the three of them - my mother, father and Eddie Cross they had systematically ground me down into the earth like I was the lowest form of life; a worm that crawled on its belly and was stomped on if it got in the way.

I turned to drugs to escape a ruthless world, and to buy drugs you have to have money - lots of it. So I begged, stole and rented out my body to raise the cash for the drug I so desperately needed.

I slept under the stars, washed in the toilets and cleaned restaurants and cafes occasionally for the food they were going to throw away; and then on one occasion I caught a fleeting glimpse of myself in a shop window.

My once brown hair was now a dull nondescript colour, my cheeks had sunken haggard-like below eyes smudged grey with fatigue and my mouth was pursed in a grim line of despair that made me look twice my age.

My very soul cried out for relief from this misery, but nobody cared.

When people saw my outward appearance they couldn't see the pain beneath and went scurrying away from me in case I contaminated them, and who could blame them.

From that moment on I lost all hope and have been on a downward slope ever since.

tumble of boisterous games and general larking about I would disappear back into the shadows.

Whether it was due to my family situation or that I just preferred my own company I have no idea, but I seem to have always been on my own.

However, the music lesson was my favourite, and even though I couldn't play a single note, I savoured the harmonious sounds that enraptured me whenever our teacher played a piece on the piano or violin.

All at once I found myself standing in the porchway that led to the entrance of the church and as I stood there rooted to the spot I allowed the music to carry all my cares away.

'What are you doing there?' a shrill female voice demanded rudely interrupting my reverie.

My eyes flew open, instantly alert as a stout, stony-faced woman bore down on me, the cherished moment gone forever and my heart sank like a stone.

'I...I was just listening to the sound of the organ,' I stammered ill at ease at her unwelcome advance.

'Well the service is over now and I'm about to lock up. I am the church warden you know,' she said smugly drawing herself up to her full height.

I didn't know, and didn't care either.

'Look at the state of you,' she said wrinkling her nose in disgust as she eyed me up and down.

'I suspect drugs are more your God, am I right,' she asked snootily raising her oddly shaped eyebrows at me.

Sighing heavily I ignored her and as she turned away I heard her say that she was leaving by the side entrance so I had better leave now.

'And may God help you,' she called out as she went back inside.

'You're right there lady,' I yelled rudely after her, and then as I felt so sick and unhappy I leant my head forward onto the frame of the door in an attitude of prayer and pleaded, 'God, if you are really there, help me ...please.'

I heard the woman bolt the door against me and through the small window I watched as she walked away, she on the inside, and me on the outside, as always.

If only that woman had been nice and welcoming but then realisation hit me, this really was the end of the road for me. While I had been standing there not quite sure what to do next, I saw to my dismay that it was snowing again.

Stumbling forward with icy flakes tearing at my face and glasses, effectively blinding me I forgot the steps and as my feet slid away from under me I crashed headlong down towards the ground slamming my head hard against something cold and stony and everything went black.

I came round spitting snow with a massive headache thumping horribly on the side of my head with all the breath knocked out of me.

Scrambling to my feet I happened to look up to see what I had obviously hit my head on.

It was a statue of Jesus with his arms outstretched.

'Oh great!' I spat in disgust, 'that's the very last time I ask you for help' and with a dramatic flourish, that nearly floored me again, I bowed irreverently before it.

'Thank you so much for nothing.'

With that I retrieved my glasses, which luckily were still intact, and stomped off as fast as my now very sore head and thickening snow would allow more certain than ever this world had no place for me in it, and the sooner I left it the better.

So much for Christian charity, that snotty woman and then hitting my head on that statue, of all things a statue of the Son of God.

It was quite clear to me now that I wasn't going to get any help so I had better just get on with it.

Peering through the curtain of snow that was now falling quite thickly I happened to see a pub on the opposite side to where I was standing and I wondered vaguely why I hadn't noticed it before. Bright lights shone through the windows and it seemed welcoming enough so I made my way hesitantly over to the entrance.

The name hung over the door in crooked back lettering: 'Ye Olde Cockleshell Inn'.

4

The Old Inn

Taking a deep breath I pushed hard on the heavy oak door which creaked loudly as it swung open.

At least I won't find God in here I thought rather smugly.

And then as I entered the distinct stench of stale beer and cigarette smoke that wafted over to me made my stomach heave and churn bringing back long ago memories that haunted me still and I had to fight back the panic that threatened to overwhelm me.

Smiling faces and the buzz of happy chatter met me as I had come in but it all died away as everyone it seemed turned to stare curiously at me.

Well, it was to be expected I suppose, I shouldn't think they saw the likes of me every day.

Feeling extremely self-conscious and ill at ease I made my way over to the bar struggling to appear more confident than I felt and sat myself up onto one of the stools there; and when the portly barman enquired what I wanted, before I could utter a single word, a man seated on my right hand side addressed him saying that a mug of hot sweet tea would probably do me the world of good.

Before I had the chance to say that maybe I didn't want tea the barman had turned away to brew it.

How dare he order for me but before I could challenge him on it all I could see was his back as he had moved away to speak to somebody nearby.

Still feeling put out but deciding it was too late to do anything about it now I gazed cautiously about the place.

At one end of the room a huge log fire burned brightly beneath an arched brick fireplace, and a group of men I gathered were mainly fishermen judging by their clothing were gathered around it in a huddle warming their frozen hands and feet.

What I would have given to sit near that fire as I was shivering constantly, and it wasn't just a physical coldness either it was as if an icy hand clutched at my heart, at my very being.

On top of the bar an artificial Christmas tree twinkled merrily and its shiny silver coloured leaves fluttered gaily every time the door was opened, but I felt as if it were mocking me as I certainly didn't feel the least bit Christmassy.

Sprigs of holly, and a bunch of mistletoe hanging discreetly in one corner; the aroma of roasting chestnuts and the low sound of festive music coming from a small radio behind the bar should all have helped to make me feel more in tune with the season but I was in too much pain and couldn't wait to see the back of it.

Disconsolately my eyes roved around the room noting the fishing nets strung across the ceiling and the highly-polished brasses gleaming on every wall.

Old oak beams were interspersed here and there with pictures of gaily-coloured fishing boats now static on small pebble beaches, and storm-lashed lighthouses under glowering black skies, all helped to make me feel very small and insignificant.

It was all so alien to everything I have been used to, I was an outsider and loneliness hugged me in its tight embrace.

However I was determined to make the most of my last night on this earth so I studied the people around me in a vain attempt to enjoy their company.

Over in one corner a couple of locals were playing a game of chess, and in-between moves they were having a fairly light-hearted argument on everything ranging from politics to lambing; while another man sat nearby holding a small black and white dog on his lap, and every so now and again, it would rear up onto its hind legs and perform tricks to the great amusement of the other customers. At the other end of the room a game of darts had just broken up amid wails of protest from one wizened old man.

'Come on you fellas,' he was saying, 'jus' one more game for the road eh?'

However, 'the fellas' had other ideas which included drinking the home-made brew dry, so in disgust the little old man came and sat up at the bar near me.

Perched there on his stool he reminded me of a small gnome, his cheeks all flushed pink, looking for all the world as if he were sat on a toadstool.

If I hadn't felt so awful I probably would have laughed but the withdrawal from my precious drug, along with the rape I had endured, the very last thing I felt like doing was laughing and now, unfortunately, whether it was due to coming in from the cold to the warmth of the pub or the bang on my head from that statue but I started to feel sick and dizzy.

My heart beat wildly in my chest and a trickle of sweat crawled uncomfortably down my back.

I had to get out of there, and fast.

As I attempted to stand up another wave sent me reeling and losing my balance I fell heavily against someone alongside me, it was the same man who had said I should have hot tea to drink.

He had obviously returned to his stool, and unfortunately I was now sprawled in a heap all over him.

Barely able to raise my head, I waited with bated breath for the cuff round the ear or a mouthful of abuse but to my great relief neither was forthcoming, and instead I was helped back onto my stool and held there until the room ceased to spin, and when I turned towards the man in gratitude I gazed blearily up into a pair of dark serious eyes that were full of concern for me.

He was fairly young, in his early thirties I'd say and long black wavy hair framed a tanned good-natured face.

'You're ill,' he said, 'come on I'll take you home, you're in no fit state.'

And without further ado, he downed the rest of his drink, paid the bill and reaching for his black jacket that was slung casually on a stool nearby he got to his feet.

He was tall and of average build but he exuded a strength that was at odds with the shabby clothing he was wearing, in fact you could almost say he looked quite scruffy and I had to admit to feeling slightly alarmed at his appearance, and almost in awe of him.

'Please, don't trouble yourself,' I exclaimed anxiously.

'I'm fine.'

'Well, you don't look fine to me and it really is no trouble,' he replied taking hold of my arm.

'What's your name?'

'It's Mike,' I answered tersely pulling my arm away roughly.

'Listen, you can barely stand and you're trembling like a leaf.'

'I'm fine,' I repeated.

'I had one too many that's all,' and with this priceless piece of wisdom on my part I saw him glance at the now cooling mug of tea in front of me, what a fool I was to think I could put one over him.

I could feel his eyes on me now assessing me, and I had the distinct impression he could see right through my façade and note the lonely, frightened boy hiding there.

Seeming to come to a decision regarding my fate, he threw me somewhat by offering his hand for me to shake.

'Very well then, if you're sure.'

Reluctantly, I reached out to grasp his proffered hand, and immediately felt a welcome heat emanating from it that engulfed me in a sensation I have never experienced before.

To be honest, it was such a wonderful feeling I was loath to let go and held on for as long as I deemed reasonably polite.

'Take care of yourself then my young friend,' and withdrawing his hand he placed it momentarily on my shoulder, and turned and left, the heavy oak door swinging shut behind him.

At his departure I felt oddly abandoned, he had been a total stranger, but there had been an air of gentleness about him, and at least he hadn't treated me with disdain like so many people I have encountered before.

Peering briefly around me, the warmth and light in there didn't feel welcoming now the man had gone and I was acutely aware of being alone and friendless again.

I'm getting soft. I told myself off crossly blinking away sudden unwanted tears, but I couldn't deny the lump in my throat as I prepared to take my leave.

5

The Man

Wandering around in the cold and dark after leaving the pub I tripped over unseen roots of trees and crashed into low-lying sharp bushes and shrubs that tore mercilessly at my face and hands in my quest to find shelter for the night.

Everything swam before my eyes and the bitterly cold air that penetrated down into my lungs made me cough painfully.

When I had almost given up hope of finding some place to stay, I came across an old, disused fishing hut and practically falling into a dry corner, I curled up into a ball shivering and gasping for breath.

As I lay there, feeling quite distraught, I became aware of the unfamiliar sound of the ringing of church bells in the distance heralding the start of the festive season; and after peering upwards through a crack in the roof I found I could see a solitary star shining brightly in the now cloudless sky.

I absolutely had no faith in any God anymore but feeling pretty desperate and sick, and needing some form of comfort, I allowed my mind to travel back in time to that stable in Bethlehem.

It would have been warm with the hot breath of the animals, and I wondered vaguely what they must have thought of these two human beings who had so rudely invaded their lives and produced a squalling babe right there in their very midst.

The young child who had grown up to be a man of great strength and courage in the face of adversity.

I longed now for the compassion he showed, not only to the Jews, but to everyone he met.

Where was he now when I needed him so badly?

Nowhere, I resigned myself.

They had been just childhood stories, and wishful thinking on my part.

That night felt as if it would never end and as the bats squeaked in my ears and red foxes called in that weird barking sound of theirs, I came to the painful conclusion that I had made the right decision.

The sheer misery and wretchedness of it all consumed me and again my throat felt tight and constricted.

Christmas Day dawned dull and freezing and even though the sky looked bleak and oppressive, thankfully no more snow had fallen during the night.

My whole body ached and unfortunately I realised that I was now suffering from 'cold turkey'.

That is the term used for the withdrawal of drug abuse; so-called as the skin starts to form little bumps on it that bear a certain resemblance to that of a cold turkey.

One minute I would burn as if on fire and the next shiver and shake with the chills; I had stomach cramps and felt as if I was going to throw up any time soon.

With a heavy heart I abandoned the comparative safety of the old hut and as I could hear and smell the sea quite close by, I tentatively made my way towards it.

I was becoming weaker and weaker with every step and as I stumbled along I panted with the exertion of trying to stay upright on the slippery ground.

My head was pounding and when great gasps of white vapour started to stream from my ever open mouth I was almost relieved when at long last the top of the cliff loomed up ahead.

Each step was agony and as I climbed higher and higher white and grey seagulls wheeled and dipped above me, and strange as it may seem, I felt as if their mewing cry came from deep within me.

At long last as I finally clawed my way up to the precipice I gazed out to sea mesmerised at the sight before me, but unhappily the water that day looked dark and unfriendly, just like a mirror of the world.

Swaying very gently in the breath of wind that ruffled my scant clothing and unkempt hair I now knew what an over-stretched elastic band ready to snap felt like, and a surge of anger swept over me as I stood there ready to jump.

How had I come to this?

Why was this the only way out for me?

Snatching my glasses away from my face I stuffed them into a pocket, I wouldn't be needing them where I was going and that thought terrified me.

But what choice did I have?

Beads of cold sweat had broken out on my forehead and upper lip and inside I was silently screaming.

My hands were clenched so tightly my broken nails pierced the soft palms causing blood to drip from them onto the icebound cliff top.

I felt crushed by my experiences - there was no hope left, and no ray of light to save me from myself.

But then I heard a man's voice:

'Don't do it Mike.'

For a moment I was thrown, I had been beaten and abused. I was cold and wet and the very last thing I needed was a spectator.

'Come away from the edge little one,' came his voice again.

Who could it be?

Nobody knew I was coming up here this morning.

Who would come out on Christmas Day in conditions like these?

And then, as if he had read my mind.

'I spoke to you in the pub last night.'

'Do you remember?'
How could I ever forget.
'W...what are you doing here?'
I was shivering so hard even my teeth were chattering.
'Looking for you.'
I couldn't believe what I was hearing.
'How did you know I w...would be up h...here?'
'Oh, just a feeling.'
'Do you always rely on your feelings,' I asked, my voice dripping with sarcasm.
'Always,' came the quick reply.
Then out of the corner of my eye I saw him take off his jacket and hold it out to me.
'You had better put this on, it's freezing up here.'
Quite rudely I ignored it.
'Go away, I don't want to live like this anymore.'
'All life is precious Mike, you can't simply throw it away.'
Anger welled up in me then.
'It's my life so I can damn well do what I like with it,' I shot back at him.
And as I shuffled ever closer to the edge I heard him take a step towards me.
'Don't come any nearer, I don't want or need your help.'
'I think maybe you need something.'
'Go away,' I screamed at him.
'I'm not going anywhere unless I take you with me.'
'You don't understand,' I muttered miserably.
'How could you?'
'I do, more than you could ever know.'
My resolve began to waver then as I recalled his gentleness, and the strange warmth that had enveloped me when we shook hands.
'Who are you anyway?'
'I'm a shepherd.'
'L...lost one of your sheep have you?'

'You could say that.'

'Will you c...carry it home on your shoulders when you find it?'

'If it will let me.'

And he spoke those words so softly I knew they were meant for me. As hot salty tears welled up in my eyes and I brushed them angrily away I heard him say, 'don't try to stop them.'

'Stop what?'

'Your tears, they were meant to be shed not bottled up inside where they can cause a lot of pain.'

'I bet you never cry.'

'I'm afraid you would lose your bet.'

'Mike...' he said, tugging gently at my sleeve.

'Come on, don't hold back.'

He was throwing me a lifeline - this man, this stranger, and I could either grab it or jump.

I grabbed it.

The closeness of this man with his calm, soothing voice was playing havoc with my insides and for a split second as I gazed back at him, the look of sympathy on his face was my undoing.

My emotions so long held in check, came bubbling up from deep within me, and with tears beginning to course down my face with a cry of anguish I fairly leapt into his waiting arms sobbing incoherently as all the pain and suffering just came pouring out of me. And as I buried my face in his chest scrabbling frantically at his clothing I clung to him terrified that at any moment he might disappear and I would be alone again. If it hadn't been for this man, taking the trouble to come and find me, I would now be lying at the bottom of the cliff, a piece of broken humanity awaiting the sea to come in and wash me away.

Of that fact I had no doubt, and as if sensing this I felt him place his old jacket around me and love seemed to flow from every fibre of it.

'It's alright Mike,' I heard him say.
'You're safe now.'
'I've got you.'

At his words my legs gave way beneath me and I collapsed, and catching me up into his strong arms as I fell he cradled me there as if I were a small child and held me tightly to him.

I had no will to resist, and as I leaned my tired head against his shoulder I briefly felt his beard brush my cheek.

'Let's go home,' he said.

And those words were music to my ears.

6

Agony

I was barely conscious but I was aware of his booted feet as he trudged away from the cliff top across the snow encrusted ground; and after what felt like an age I heard him enter a small house or cottage and then carry me into a room where I could hear the crackle and hiss of an open fire. Laying me down gently onto a rug already placed there in front of it I was immediately bathed in a comforting warmth.

Then as I watched through half-closed eyes, I saw him remove his boots and cross the bare wooden floor on silent feet.

I must have passed out as the next thing I knew I had been covered with an old brown blanket that had been tucked firmly around me but underneath I was naked apart from my pants.

Panic surged through me.

The man had been standing by the window looking out with his back to me but turned when he heard me stir.

Consternation crossed his face as he realised what was happening and in two strides he was down on the floor beside me.

'Be still my young friend, be still, I won't hurt you.'

Then to my horror, I began to hyperventilate clawing at my face with my nails as my heart threatened to explode inside me.

Without attempting to touch me he then in a calm soothing voice encouraged me to take slow deep breaths until eventually the beating of my heart slowed to a more natural rhythm and letting out a long sigh of relief I let my arms fall to my sides in an attitude of resignation.

'I had no choice but to remove your clothing,' he spoke almost apologetically.

'You were shivering so hard and your clothes were so wet, I couldn't leave you like that.'

'What happened to you Mike?'

'Your pants are ripped and covered in blood.'

How could I tell him what had been done to me, as it was I was consumed with guilt at not having put up much of a fight.

I had let them hurt me and I was mortified.

Such was my anguish I wanted the floor to open up and swallow me.

How I wished I hadn't been persuaded not to jump off that cliff then all this suffering would be over.

Realising I was still shivering either from the cold or more likely shock he said that maybe a hot drink would be a good idea and with that he disappeared into a room at the back.

While I waited for him to return I gazed around me at my surroundings.

The room was relatively small with only a few sticks of furniture that I could see from my vantage point on the floor.

An armchair stood either side of the fireplace with what looked like a hand-made stool for drinks, and by the window stood a medium-sized table with two chairs.

Remarkably there were no photos or pictures of any kind and the room didn't really feel 'lived-in.'

But then, what with him being a shepherd, he probably wouldn't be interested in that sort of thing anyway, quite a lonely life I mused, being a shepherd.

When he arrived back carrying a steaming mug that had the distinct aroma of hot chocolate about it he bent down and placed the drink to my lips, however I turned my face away, I don't really know why.

He wasn't about to put up with that though and kneeling on the floor behind me he raised me up so that I was half-lying on his lap, and somehow he managed to coax me into drinking it.

Hot chocolate has never tasted so good, but I wasn't about to tell him that.

As I finished the drink and he had placed the now empty mug on the table by the window he suggested that maybe he should clean me up a bit and crouching down beside me he pulled the blanket away from my top half and I cringed in terror.

On seeing this reaction he quickly tucked the blanket back around me again.

'You have been in the wars haven't you young one,' he said brushing the hair away from my forehead with gentle fingers.

'I'll go and get some warm water and hopefully make you feel more comfortable...and we will take it slowly,' he added, patting my arm as he stood up.

He soon returned holding a steaming bowl, a cloth, towel and some jars I assumed were ointments of some kind.

Watching my reaction the whole time he then gingerly removed the blanket and somehow I managed to stay calm.

Bathing my chest and stomach with the soft cloth and drying me off with the towel as he went, he then turned his attention to my arms, and when he came across the needle marks he ran the tips of his fingers over them unhappily making me feel decidedly uncomfortable.

When he had finished with my front he then lifted me up so he could get to my back and I briefly felt him lay a hand on my now very sore shoulder, and if there had been a fly on the wall it couldn't fail to have noticed that the wound was now no longer there.

Once my top half was reasonably clean, he applied some ointment to the cuts and a liquid to the bruises which was very soothing. However, the rape had been brutal and I knew they'd torn me for I had felt blood oozing from my backside for a while now and the pain of it was becoming unbearable, and so as I fidgeted in a vain attempt to ease the distress I was in the man noticed and nodding towards my lower regions asked if it would be alright if he took a look.

As I remained silent I guess he thought I was in agreement so asking me to turn over onto my side he then pulled the waistband of my pants away from my lower back so he could see properly and immediately in a shocked voice he asked,

'What's been going on here?'

And as I glanced fearfully back at him I watched his face darken as he came to realise exactly what had taken place.

'You poor boy, who did this to you?'

The degradation of it all consumed me, my mind in such torment.

Sighing heavily he said something about fetching some fresh water, but unfortunately after he had gone dark thoughts began to surface in my befuddled brain.

Why was he going to all this trouble?

Who was he anyway?

A shepherd?

Yeah right, haven't seen any sheep yet.

Why would he come out to find me when nobody else had bothered or even cared?

Was it because he wanted me for himself?

In my experience nobody did anything for nothing.

He would want recompense.

As he arrived back, an anger mixed with a heightened anxiety built up within me until it reached fever pitch, and then it all spilled out with a venom that frightened me.

Taking hold of my ripped pants I tore them off leaving me starkers.

'Go on then!'

'Here I am!'

'Take me for yourself,' I yelled at him crying and choking in my anguish.

A look of complete shock flew across his bewildered face.

'You're not doing all this for nothing, you want me don't you.'

His silence was deafening.

And then with his voice cracking with emotion he spoke the words that filled me with dismay.

'Mike...I can see for myself how much you have suffered and I am truly sorry for that.

However hard this will be, I would like you to be able to accept my compassion in the spirit that it is meant.

I mean you no harm and I certainly don't want you to debase yourself, the only thing I want from you, is your trust.'

And then after a long pause, as he let his words sink in, he asked if I wanted him to continue, or if I preferred, he could take me up to the cottage hospital and they would look after me.

To be honest I was stunned and for a moment didn't know what to say.

I certainly didn't want to go to any hospital and I also felt now that I really didn't have much choice in the matter.

I felt like such a fool, he had only wanted to help me out of the goodness of his heart and I had flung it back at him most cruelly.

'I would prefer you to continue...if that's alright with you,' I answered in a trembling voice.

'I am not your enemy Mike, I just want to help you... that's all.

Well alright then, if you would roll over onto your side again and face the fire I'll try and make this as easy as possible for you.'

Turning back onto my side as he requested I watched uneasily as the flames crackled and licked their way up the chimney, but I needn't have worried.

His hands were warm and gentle as he bathed my backside with a sensitivity I didn't think a man could possess.

After all the sadistic men I have encountered, his empathy for me was a revelation.

And when he placed some ointment there and covered it with a pad of some kind shame and a deep self-loathing made my face burn.

My experiences had turned me into something hateful when I couldn't even recognise genuine concern, and feeling like a wounded animal I had been ready to bite the hand that fed me and I was aghast at how low I had sunk.

And then in the midst of my self-pitying I could hardly believe it when I felt a comforting hand on my arm, and I was grateful for this silent gesture.

As I rolled onto my back again as he finished, the orange glow flickering from the fire illuminated the man's face as he diligently bathed my legs and feet and I became aware of small, uneven scars spread across his forehead, and I wondered about them.

After he had finished he picked me up effortlessly and carried me over to a bed in a corner of the room I hadn't noticed before, and after covering me up with warm blankets I heard him clearly say,

'Sleep now little one, and be still.
God is watching.'

And one day, those words would come back to haunt me.

7

A Helping Hand

At first I managed to drift off into a dreamless slumber. My respite didn't last long though and as to be expected, the effects of going 'cold turkey' reared their ugly heads and I was overcome with horrendous nightmares and the stomach cramps returned with a vengeance.

Fever made me toss and turn relentlessly and sweat poured from my body soaking the sheet I was lying on.

Punching off the bedclothes I writhed and moaned, scrunching myself up into a tight ball begging for release from this hell.

In my distress I must have cried out because when I opened my eyes the man was there seated beside me wiping my brow with a cool cloth willing me silently to be patient and hold on.

This would pass.

Knowing he was close by comforted me somewhat but sleep evaded me now and instead I was being sick and I had diarrhoea which for the man must have been most unpleasant as he spent half his time cleaning me up.

I lost track of time over the next few days and nights - it just seemed to blur into a sea of pain that was nothing like I had ever experienced before.

I remember one particularly bad moment in the middle of the night when I was restless and agitated and in such torment with the stomach cramps that made me nauseous.

I was clutching at my stomach so hard and had really started to believe that death would be preferable to this when the covers were lifted off me and I felt a hand easing its way through my clenched arms and resting eventually on my now throbbing body.

A warmth flowed from this hand and it spread over me like a comfort blanket, and ever so slowly the awful griping pain inside me began to subside until my whole being relaxed and went limp with relief.

Thankfully, I now slept like a baby.

I had turned a corner.

Later, I came to realise that the man's hands on my bruised and battered body had healed me in so many more ways than one, and I would be forever grateful.

8

A Woodworker?

I awoke to see a shaft of sunlight filtering through a gap in the curtains and falling upon the face of the man who was fast asleep in the chair beside my bed.

He must have only been half-asleep as he immediately opened his eyes, looked at me, and smiled.

'Good morning,' he said, 'how are you feeling?'

'Better...um I think,' I answered warily.

'How long have I been lying here?'

'Mm, about four days.'

'Oh boy,' I gasped.

'Are you hungry?'

I thought about that for a bit and then realised that I was.

'That's good.'

And then, as an afterthought, 'maybe you would like a bath first?'

'Sure, why not.'

'I'll go and run it for you,' he said, getting to his feet.

Stretching and yawning loudly I couldn't believe how well I felt, and then, climbing slowly out of bed and covering myself with one of the blankets, I went over to the window and drew the curtains aside.

The breath caught in my throat as I gazed at the sight before me.

The sea.

In all my wildest dreams I could never have imagined anything so incredible.

The mix of colours was awesome - deepest blue, emerald green and here and there hints of lavender and even darkest navy.

It was stunning.

And as the waves rippled lazily onto the shore white foam bubbled and fizzed over the top of them completing an almost idyllic picture.

Such a contrast from when it appeared so dark and menacing when I had been almost going out of my mind with terror.

Unlatching the window a gust of pure, clean salty air hit me full in the face and I laughed at the sheer joy of it all.

When the man arrived back he couldn't have failed to notice the pleasure on my face as I turned to him grinning from ear to ear.

'The bath is waiting for you, but don't be too long as breakfast will be ready soon.'

He was trying to be stern and that he hadn't seen how gloriously happy I was but a slight smile at the corners of his mouth gave him away.

'It's good to be alive Mike, don't ever forget that.'

And then, recalling how traumatic the last few days had been and how if it hadn't been for this man...

As I stood there looking up into his kind face such a wave of emotion swept over me that I was compelled to reach out and grab him in a bear hug, and leaning against him I cried, not with sadness but gratitude, and I felt his arms come around my back to comfort me as I knew they would.

Of course in the midst of all this my blanket fell to the floor and my nakedness was exposed again, but I didn't care. He had asked me to trust him and I hadn't been sure, but now I was.

Realising I probably stunk to high heaven I reluctantly pulled away from him, but he either hadn't noticed or didn't care.

'Sorry about that,' I said embarrassed.

'No need,' he said, noting my discomfort, 'better out than in.'

'Yes,' I said, trying to smile through my tears.

'I remember.'

'Better go for that bath,' he remarked, ducking down and retrieving the fallen blanket and placing it gently around me, 'I wouldn't like you to get sick again just when you are starting to get better.'

I nodded in agreement.

'Go now,' and he pointed in the direction of the bathroom.

As I lay soaking in the hot soapy water I started to enjoy the sensation of being really clean at long last; and I uttered a small whisper of thanks to nobody in particular, that I had been saved.

The man had left me some clothes, his I assumed from when he was younger, but they still swamped my skeletal frame.

'Hm, we will have to see about getting you some new clothes,' he remarked as I came back buttoning up a shirt that hung on me.'

He was already seated at the table with two steaming bowls of porridge waiting to be eaten.

'Come,' he said, indicating the chair opposite him.

As I sat down, and went to pick up my spoon, I noticed that he had bent his head over his bowl and was saying something under his breath.

'What did you say,' I asked.

'I was thanking God for the food.'

'Oh yes, of course,' I said far too quickly to be sincere.

'You don't believe?'

'No, I don't.'

He went quiet for a moment and then, 'eat your porridge, you want to get well again don't you?'

And I dutifully nodded.

Thereafter, before every meal he thanked God for it which I thought was a bit weird but, hey-ho if that's what rings his bell then that was ok by me.

When we had finished eating and cleared away the dishes he suggested I sit by the fire for a while as he had some work to do.

'I thought you said you were a shepherd, there are no sheep in here,' I remarked cheekily.

'I have sheep everywhere,' he replied, 'but today I am a woodworker and must mend a broken table.'

Leaving me sitting in one of the big, old armchairs I watched as he went over to a space he had made in one corner of the room.

There were many different shaped tools hanging on the wall and inside a cupboard many boxes of nails and screws were piled on top of each other, while a small broken-down table stood alongside looking quite forlorn awaiting his attention.

'So you do carpentry as well then,' I asked.

'Among other things.'

'A sort of Jack-of-all trades?'

'Something like that.'

I studied him as he worked, stripping bits off here and adding bits there, and even though I was no expert I could tell he was no amateur.

After a couple of hours when I was beginning to get bored he announced that the table was now fit for purpose and that he was going to return it to its owner.

'Where do they live?' I enquired hoping it wasn't too far away so I could accompany him.

'In the village,' he said, putting on his jacket and boots and hefting the table onto his shoulder.

'Can I come too?'

'It's a fair walk, do you think you're up to it?'

'I'm up to it,' and I fairly leapt out of the chair eager to stand beside him.

'Let's go then,' he said, noting my enthusiasm.

'Put on that old coat and that pair of boots,' and he indicated where his had been.

'You're going to need them even if they are too big for you.'

Doing as he requested I then joined him outside. It was brilliantly sunny but icily cold and I hugged the coat around me.

He strode ahead a picture of health and well-being and I almost had to run to keep up with him.

When he finally noticed I was struggling he was apologetic and teasing all at the same time.

'I was forgetting that you are just a wee lad.'

I threw him a disgusted look punching him playfully on the arm and he laughed, a wonderful deep-throated sound that was a real pleasure to hear.

After feeling like death warmed up the last few days bizarrely I actually felt really well for the first time in years.

'Where are we going exactly?'

'Tired?'

'No, I just wondered that's all.'

'Grocers shop up the road here run by a lovely Indian couple - Mr. and Mrs. Singh.'

9

A Shock

As we trudged along on the now compacted snow I happened to become aware of a boy on the other side of the road keeping pace with us.

He looked about my age but could have been older, and he kept giving me dirty looks as if to say I shouldn't be there.

As he was starting to make me nervous I asked the man about him.

'Yes, I see him, his name is Benny.'

'What's his problem?'

'Boredom I should think, he left school under a cloud, and of course, now he is having trouble finding someone who will give him a job. There isn't much employment around here so he really needs to venture into the big towns.'

'I hope he's not looking for trouble.'

'Don't worry,' he said, glancing my way, 'I will look after you.'

And then, as luck would have it, I lost my footing on a lump of ice and instinctively made a grab for the man's arm.

The boy sniggered and I felt my face burn with humiliation.

It was quite a relief to finally reach the grocers shop and to watch as our 'shadow' carried on walking.

As we entered a little bell announced our arrival and the woman at the counter beamed happily at us.

'Good morning Mrs. Singh, how are you today?'

'Well hello, I'm fine thank you, how are you?'

It was fairly quiet at the moment as it was only about twelve o'clock so we found an empty table and reached for a menu.

'Decided what you would like yet,' he enquired after studying the various meals on offer.

'Yes, I think I should like shepherd's pie, I always liked that.'

'Anything else?'

'No, I don't think so,' and then rummaging around in my trousers pocket in search of the roll of money I had taken off the floor in that basement flat I felt quite deflated when it appeared to be missing, completely forgetting that my old clothes had probably been thrown away.

I wondered briefly if the man had found it but I knew without a shadow of a doubt he would have mentioned it.

'I don't have any money to help pay for the meal,' I stated feeling quite dejected.

'Not a problem, I think I will have the same.'

As he went up to the counter to place our order a cold blast of air made me shiver as someone entered.

It was our 'shadow' from earlier on and he wasn't alone, he had two other boys with him.

When they passed by our table they gave it a bit of a shove as if to say, 'we're here, be very afraid.'

They sat down close by, making me feel quite intimidated.

Completely oblivious to the boys who were now causing me to shake with anxiety, the man came back and sat down again.

'Anything wrong,' he asked, noting my agitation.

'No, I'm fine thanks,' I lied.

We sat in silence for a bit and then I thought I would broach the subject of who he really was.

'I've been thinking.'

'Oh yes.'

'I know what you do for a living and that you're a shepherd of sorts although I've yet to see any sheep, but what is your name?'

'What should I call you?'

A pained expression fleetingly crossed his face as he answered.

'I've been called many things.'

'Such as?'

'You really don't want to know.'

'Yes I do.'

'What is your birth name?'

'What did your parents call you?'

Here he gave me a searching look and then stunned me by saying:

'It's Yeshua.'

'Ok...' I said, slowly digesting what he had just said.

'But that's Jewish for Jesus isn't it?'

He smiled.

'Uh huh.'

'You're making fun of me now, come on really, what is your real name?'

'That is my real name.'

'Alright, then I am Robin Hood,' I said, pulling a face.

'You don't believe me.'

'Of course I don't, why would I, you can't possibly be called Jesus. Who would want to be called Jesus?'

'I would, because...I am.'

'You're trying to tell me that you have the same name as a dead carpenter who lived and died nearly two thousand years ago.'

'No, I'm saying that I am He.'

I was gobsmacked and angry at this obvious lie.

'You can't possibly be Jesus - he's dead.'

'If you recall I came back to life three days later.'

He looked so sincere but I just knew he was mocking me. But why?

Why would he lie about a thing like that?

'Ok, ok so you are trying to tell me that *you* are the Son of God'.

My hackles were up now and I was livid.

'Then, if you are who you say you are, what are you doing down here in lowly Cornwall?'

'I came for you.'

'For me?'

I was now well and truly flummoxed and starting to feel as if I were in some kind of weird dream.

'But...but that's ridiculous. Why would you care about me of all people?'

'Why not you?'

'Listen, I'm a regular scumbag; I've stolen, taken drugs and been a rent boy for money...' and here my voice trailed away in shame.

'I'm not worthy.'

'Well,' and here he reached out a hand and placed it comfortingly on my shoulder before continuing.

'You cried out for help, and I heard you.'

'What, when?'

'Just after you had been shut out of the church, remember?'

'Oh, oh yes, I remember, but I didn't really believe I would get any help. All the time people out there are asking for help, so I ask again, why me?'

'Everyone is heard, but you.. You were alone in a dark sea of misery and despair, a lamb lost in the wilderness.'

'Tell me,' and here he tilted his head to one side and looked directly at me.

'How could I leave you like that? So I chose to come and find you.'

And that word, 'chose' rang a bell in my brain.

Whenever I had been plagued by the bullies at school I would often retreat to the library.

Along with music I loved to read and books became a form of escapism I needed so badly; and I even read the bible, well some of it anyway.

Poetry especially was a great help and a source of inspiration, especially the poems written during the two world wars; and around this time I happened to come across a poem about the crucifixion and the last verse, if I can remember it correctly, went like this:

Were you there when he rose
Did you see how he chose
To love us I suppose.

Did he really choose to come because he loved me?

Raising my head, my stomach in knots, I studied him.

He certainly looked the part with the long dark hair, beard and his eyes...I had to admit they did speak only of love.

He was so earnest but I felt, probably unfairly, that he was just too good to be true.

But how could he be Jesus?

I certainly wasn't convinced, after all it was too ridiculous for words.

It was laughable except I didn't feel like laughing.

I knew undoubtedly though, there was something strange about him and he had been unbelievably kind to me, but to suggest He was the Son of God was really a stretch too far.

He was surely playing with my mind and I didn't like it one little bit.

When our food arrived we ate it in an uncomfortable silence, and I felt as if I was going to choke on every mouthful.

I finished first and unable to stand the tension any longer, I stood up so abruptly I sent my chair flying and after returning it to the table I fled as quickly as I could.

Unperturbed he countered with, 'this young man is my friend and is in my care, anything you wish to say to him you say to me instead,' and his voice held a hint of authority to it.

I couldn't see what was happening as the man was a lot taller than me, but I came to realise he was in effect shielding me from them.

He had called me his friend a couple of times now and my heart swelled with pride.

They seemed to back off, but then out of the blue, the one called Benny took a flying leap and sent the man crashing to the ground in front of me.

I knew he was fairly strong but he had been unprepared for the kick and losing his balance had fallen heavily onto his side.

To be honest I was paralyzed with fear and didn't know whether to summon up the courage to help him or to run for help.

As he lay motionless on the freezing ground all three of them began kicking him in the ribs and stomach and to my amazement he just took it without even attempting to retaliate or roll away from them.

Finally, I summoned up the courage to yell at them to stop but they then turned on me as well, pushing me to the ground and laughing scornfully.

'What a pair of jelly babies,' one of them hissed, 'come on guys, let's leave these two weaklings, I can't be bothered with them,' and they swaggered off sniggering loudly at the tops of their voices.

Getting to my feet I helped the man up who was holding his side and breathing heavily.

'Are you alright?' I asked, realising that he wasn't.

'I'm fine,' he managed to gasp.

'How about you?'

'I'm okay.'

'I thought you said there was no need to worry.'

'Well, we're alright aren't we?'

'I am, but I'm not so sure about you.'

'It could have been a lot worse.'

'Why didn't you hit him back or at least say something,' I asked feeling quite perplexed.

'What good would that have done?'

'Well, it would have shown them that you weren't afraid, nobody likes to be called a coward.'

'Is that what you think I am - a coward?'

'No, I suppose not, but you could have at least slapped one of them or if you are who you say you are,' I ridiculed him, 'you could probably have turned them to stone or something.'

'Is that what you think I should have done?'

'Yes,' I yelled back at him, embarrassed that neither one of us had retaliated.

'Well, that's not my way, and if I had hit one of them then all three would have jumped on us and we would have come off much worse than we are now.'

'Besides giving tit for tat is not the answer, violence has never and will never solve anything, it would just have made us as bad as them.

Am I right?'

I thought about that for about two seconds and had to concede that he was.

'I guess so, but I wish I'd had the courage to punch one of them.'

'Well, I'm glad you didn't, don't forget that an eye for an eye is not the answer.'

'What is then against bullies like that?' 'Well...' he considered, 'don't go and hide, but stand your ground and embrace the fear'.

'And if all else fails,' he added with a twinkle in his eye. 'Run!'

'You could have run,' I retorted, wanting to hurt him.

'What, when?'

'You know when you were in that garden just before they came for you.'

I don't really know why I was goading him, especially as I hadn't believed a word he had told me about who he was.

'No, I had to let them take me,' he said, brushing himself down.

'Why?'

'It was necessary.'

'Well,' I announced dramatically, snatching up the bag of muffins that had luckily escaped unscathed.

'I don't like the feeling of being a coward.'

'You know, there is a very fine line between being a coward and a hero,' he said.

And wincing in pain, he led me away and then stunned me by saying, 'maybe you could find it in your heart to feel sorry for those boys, they have so much emptiness inside them and they fill that void up with a darkness that does neither them or anyone else any good'.

On the way back, as I pondered on his words, I reflected that if it hadn't been for the man's restraint we could now quite easily be badly beaten and so reluctantly, I came to the conclusion that he had been right.

11

We toasted the muffins in front of the fire that night and when they were ready we spread butter and honey thickly on top of them, I don't think I have ever tasted anything that tasted so good.

We had left the curtains open as the night sky was a picture to behold.

Being totally cloudless a large full moon had risen and could clearly be seen reflected in all its glory in the calm lapping ocean; while it seemed like millions of stars, not overshadowed by the lights of any nearby town, sparkled and shone like exquisite diamonds in the inky black sky.

We sat either side of the fireplace in the big old armchairs mostly in companionable silence until the man said he fancied a hot chocolate and would I like one.

I agreed that would be nice and he diligently disappeared into the kitchen at the back.

It left me wondering why, if he was who he said he was, he didn't just conjure it up like in the story of the loaves and fishes when he had fed thousands of people on such a meagre amount of food.

I asked him as much when he returned holding two steaming mugs in his hands.

'There is a practical side to me as well you know, and besides, there are not thousands of people here, just you and me.'

I duly digested this.

'You're not really, 'Him' are you,' and it was a statement not a question.

Placing the hot drinks onto the small stool set before us he then promptly sat down, rolled up his sleeves and showed me his hands.

I gasped.

Not knowing what else to do I ate the porridge which was disgusting but at least the tea was ok. After I'd finished I cleared away the dishes and pondered on what I should do next.

I mooched about for a bit and then decided to go for a walk, if I was lucky I might even bump into him.

The village seemed the obvious place to aim for so donning the old coat and boots I had worn previously I stepped outside and slammed the front door. I had no way of locking it but there was nothing of value in there anyway.

It felt slightly warmer that morning and the snow underfoot had begun to melt making it slushy and hard going.

The hazy sunshine and the singing of the birds lifted my spirits somewhat and I started to enjoy the uphill walk.

When I reached my destination I browsed around the shops for a while still speculating on where the man had got to.

Eventually, when I was becoming bored, I espied a small crowd of people huddled around an elderly woman listening intently to what she was saying.

She appeared to be in a bit of a daze so just for something to do and out of curiosity I joined the group and listened in.

She was speaking so quietly I almost had to crane my neck to be able to hear her.

It seemed she had been a passenger on a coach trip to London for a weekend treat and on the return journey late last night the driver had skidded on a patch of ice and had lost control of the vehicle; and unfortunately it had careered across the road and had ended up on its side in a ditch.

'The windows smashed on impact,' she was saying, 'and flying glass had caused terrible injuries and we were all covered in blood as you can see,' and she indicated the dark red stains on her clothing, but strangely I couldn't see any cuts or even bruises of any kind on her face or hands.

'We all looked to the driver for help but he was slumped over the steering wheel having been knocked out with a terrible gash on the side of his head.

A couple of us tried to open the door but it was jammed solid and we couldn't budge it, and in our distress we didn't think to look for another exit,' she exclaimed tearfully.

'Then, just as we were envisioning having to spend the night stuck there in that stricken vehicle and panic was beginning to set in, a tall man appeared at one of the broken windows. Having managed to remove the remaining shards of glass left in the framework he then pulled us all out through the hole he had made; and then scrambling inside, he rescued the driver who was by now starting to regain consciousness.

Shock made itself felt once we were all outside and as we stood there crying and shivering as luck would have it a lone police car returning from a late night job pulled up alongside us, and after assessing the situation radioed in for assistance.

Soon a fleet of ambulances arrived and ferried us all to the local hospital where the wonderful doctors and nurses cleaned us up and gave us hot mugs of tea to drink.'

She paused here to take a shuddering breath as her eyes filled with tears and overflowing coursed down her lined cheeks; and then, when her chin began to wobble we watched horrified as she made a concerted effort to control herself.

'Now comes the extraordinary part of my tale,' she said sniffing loudly and someone kindly passed her a handkerchief and wiping her nose and eyes with a hand that visibly shook she thanked the person and continued on with her story in almost a whisper so inevitably we had to strain to hear what she was saying.

'I never would have believed it if I hadn't witnessed it myself.

Our clothes were bloodied but the medical staff were unable to find injuries of any kind on any of us.

No cuts, bruises and even the driver, nothing.

Of course, we thought they were crazy so we felt each other's arms and legs and every limb was intact; and amazingly the awful cut on the driver's head had also disappeared. This morning we all walked out of that hospital with not even a scratch on any of us.'

Someone went for a chair for her then as she looked as if she were about to fall, but when it arrived she declined it saying, 'thank you kindly, but I am going home now to get some much needed sleep, as you can well imagine, I am very tired.'

A burly man stepped forward then and offered to escort her home.

'No, thank you kindly, if I can survive a coach crash and live to tell the tale I am quite sure I can make it home by myself,' and as she made to walk away she stopped dead in her tracks when someone asked,

'What happened to the man then?'

'Oh...' and turning towards the questioner her face suddenly lit up making her look years younger.

'We never saw him again, he just seemed to vanish back into the shadows or wherever it was he had come from, but I so wish that I'd had the chance to thank him for what he did for us that night. Without a doubt we wouldn't have survived as it was terribly cold and we were all so hurt.

We were in such a state, but then, when he touched us...'

And here she paused to wipe away a tear. 'His hands,' she continued in a shaky voice, 'were warm and comforting, and it was such a wonderful feeling…

Later on, when we congregated outside with no injuries of any kind on any of us we felt that we had been rescued and healed by an angel of some kind, and as long as I live I will never forget him.'

'Did he say anything,' someone queried.

'Not a dicky bird, but then he didn't have to did he.'

And as she moved off with a ghost of a smile on her face I walked away as well my mind in a whirl.

Had it been...could it have been…?

They had all been healed of their injuries before they even reached the hospital.

It didn't make any sense unless...

As I made my way back to the cottage a chill wind blew up chasing black ominous looking clouds inland threatening either rain or more snow.

A clap of thunder shook the air and as I hurried along I wrapped the old coat around me needing to get back and to some much needed shelter.

All at once, as a bolt of lightning streaked across the sky I saw him standing there outside, his tall dark shape silhouetted against the backdrop of the dazzling light, but he was seemingly lost in thought and oblivious to the storm.

He was standing perfectly still with his arm outstretched and on the palm of his hand perched a small bird, a robin I think, and it was pecking away happily at what I presumed were breadcrumbs.

He must have heard me coming and when he turned towards me I could see that he looked tired but peaceful, unfortunately as I approached the bird took fright and flew away.

'Don't look so disheartened,' he said softly, rubbing his hands together to let the remaining crumbs fall to the ground.

'She will come back, as you have.'

'I've come back,' I replied testily.

'It's you that's been out all night.'

He chuckled.

'Well, since I've returned at least I've seen that you made some porridge.

Well done'.

'Even though it was like mush,' I said sheepishly.

He laughed.

'At least you tried.'

And then he added, 'practice makes perfect you know.'

'Well, if you think I'm making breakfast every morning,' I declared hotly, 'you are sadly mistaken.'

As we made our way inside out of the way of the storm I asked him what he planned to do that day.

'I have some work to do up at the big house on the hill.'

'Can I come too?'

'I was going to suggest it, after all you might learn something but I must have a wash first though.'

Recalling that he hadn't had any breakfast I wondered out loud if he wanted anything to eat or drink.

'No, I'm fine thanks.'

While he was gone I reflected on the fact that it probably had been him at that accident but as he hadn't volunteered any information about where he was all night I felt I should leave well alone.

13

Maisie

As we made our way up the hill large droplets of rain began to fall and we were soon soaked through.

After we arrived the man rang the bell and when the lady of the house answered he apologised for the state we were in.

'That's no problem,' and she smiled wearily and for a moment the lines of worry that had been etched on her once youthful face smoothed out and she looked almost pretty.

'Please, come in and I will bring some towels so you can dry yourselves.'

As we stepped inside onto the highly polished parquet floor and removed our coats that dripped rainwater everywhere he gave me a look that spoke volumes.

We were like drowned rats and highly undesirable visitors.

She duly came back with the towels that were warm and soft and we dried ourselves off the best we could.

'It's this way,' she announced and we followed her into a large spacious living room that was light and airy from a large window that took up almost the whole of one wall that overlooked the village and coastline.

A strategically placed blue armchair stood squarely in front of it while the rest of the highly expensive antique furniture was placed against the walls leaving the chair quite isolated.

The woman then led the man over to an old brown dresser that seemed totally out of place amidst all this luxury.

'It was my mother's and not worth anything but I could never part with it for sentimental reasons obviously.'

'Obviously,' the man smiled at her and she blushed, avoiding his eyes.

He was a good-looking man and I had the feeling she was lonely.

She sighed quietly and then said that she had better make sure that her daughter was alright and turned to go over to the chair by the window.

'I'll leave you to it then,' she exclaimed, 'if you need anything don't hesitate to ask.'

The man set to work spreading a small sheet onto the carpet to catch any mess he might make and then laid his tools neatly on top.

I could see she was suitably impressed.

'Would you care to sit here with my daughter,' she asked me realising that I felt rather like a spare wheel.

'Oh, um, yes of course,' I replied.

'Where is she?'

'She's here,' she said, tapping the armchair.

'What's your name,' she enquired.

'It's Mike.'

'Well, Mike, please come and meet Maisie.'

As I reached the chair I was shocked to see a pitifully thin girl possibly around my age half-lying awkwardly amid a swathe of cushions in an attempt to keep her upright.

I mean I was skinny but she was skeletal. Her skin was white and so thinly stretched over her bony forehead the blue veins showed through, and her eyes were closed as if it took too much effort to keep them open.

'Maisie is anorexic,' her mother informed me, observing that I was shocked.

'It's an eating disorder that makes her not want to eat anything, and I mean anything,' she stressed.

'Can't they do anything for her,' I asked, 'some pills or something,' I gabbled not knowing what to say.

'Unfortunately not, Maisie is too far gone now even though I have tempted her with every food under the sun.'

'I am still here you know Mother,' the girl unexpectedly spoke in barely an audible whisper, 'there is nothing wrong with my hearing.'

'I'm sorry my darling,' the woman sniffed and wiping away a tear stroked the dull lifeless hair on the girl's forehead as she did so.

I had the feeling that the mother had been dealing with this horrendous situation for a long time now and, understandably, was at her wits end.

At this point the phone rang.

'I must go and answer that,' she announced suitably apologetic.

'Would you keep an eye on Maisie for me please,' and she rushed from the room I felt with a certain relief from this uncomfortable conversation.

'I don't need you to keep an eye on me,' she muttered through gritted teeth.

And I could imagine the underlying anger seething within her delicate frame.

'It's ok,' I said, 'I can understand how you feel at being treated like an invalid, I would feel exactly the same way.'

'Would you,' she asked.

'You have no idea what this is like.'

'No, I don't suppose I do, especially as I have never heard of such an awful illness.'

'I had never heard of it before either, it was just that as I thought I looked so fat I decided to cut down a bit, but then it got out of hand and I ended up not wanting to eat at all.'

'But don't you get hungry,' I queried.

The slow shake of her head upset me more than I can say.

The colour of her hair looked as if it had once been blonde and I could well have imagined her at one time as being quite pretty with small features and a delicate nose,

Her mother returned just as we were heading for the front door.

'I'm sorry I was so long, you've finished then?'

'Yes, good as new now, but you had better see for yourself.'

'Oh, I'm sure there's no need.'

'How much do I owe you?'

'Just a couple will suffice thank you.'

'Are you sure, you have been here a while, maybe you should have more.'

'No, it's fine.'

As she gave him the money she thanked me for looking after Maisie.

'No problem at all,' and I smiled genially at her.

'She's a great girl.'

'Yes, she is,' she agreed.

As we turned to leave he then shocked the poor woman by saying that maybe some soup for her daughter would be a good idea.

'What, are you being funny,' she asked, obviously annoyed.

And then a small voice piped up from inside.

'Mum, I'm hungry.

What is there to eat?'

I have never seen a woman move so fast as she slammed the front door and rushed back inside.

'Oh my darling girl.

What would you like?'

14

I was pleased to see the rain had stopped while we had been in the house and instead a thick sea mist had come inland.

As we started to make our way back down the hill the man asked me if I had discovered anything about myself, and it only took me a moment to realise that I had.

'Yes, I found that I could feel sorry for someone other than myself. I had become very self-centred because I was hurting so much.'

'I think that is totally understandable, but I'm glad you could find pity in your heart for Maisie.'

'Will she ever recover, do you think? Only I heard her calling for food as we left and surely that is a good sign.'

'I'm certain she will,' and he sounded so sure that I turned to look at him and there was such a determined look on his face.

'I feel quite bad as I didn't get a chance to say goodbye to her.'

'I wouldn't worry, she won't forget you in a hurry, you did alright in there.'

'Do you really think so?'

'I know so.'

And then, quite out of the blue, he threw me completely by starting to run.

'Beat you to the bottom Mike,' and with his arms outstretched and his tool bag swinging crazily in one hand he charged back the way we had come, his jacket flapping wildly as he ran.

'What... wait', I called after him, 'you're completely mad do you know that.'

'So I've been told,' he sang out, and as he looked back over his shoulder at me the joy on his face was infectious so I tore after him arms wide the same as him, and with the cold damp air on my face my hair streaming out behind me and the sound of my boots pounding on the ground it was exhilarating.

I was flying!

We were a couple of crazy idiots running as if there were no tomorrow, and it was wonderful.

Eventually, I lost sight of him as he disappeared into the mist so as I reached the bottom of the hill I began to slow down.

Good job I did as Mr. Singh had come out of his shop and was looking in my direction.

'Hello Mr. Singh,' I panted.

'Did you want me?'

'Oh yes I'm glad I've caught you,' he said, smiling brightly.

'The clothes you were wearing the other day seemed a mite too big for you so I took the liberty of raking out my son's old clothes he has grown out of and thought you might like to have them.

If you wait here a minute I'll get them for you,' and without another word he hurried back into his shop.

Just seconds later he reappeared carrying a large brown paper parcel tied up with string.

'Here you are,' he said, 'hope you don't mind.'

'Not at all, it was very kind of you to think of me,' and to be honest I was quite blown away at this sudden generosity.

As he made no attempt to walk away I thought I should engage him in conversation.

'Your back seems to be a lot better than when I last saw you.'

'Oh my boy, it is and I feel years younger too, ever since...' and here his voice trailed away as he peered down the road after the man who had now come to a halt and was standing idly waiting for me to catch up.

Thankfully the mist had now lifted and he could be seen quite clearly.

'Tell me,' Mr. Singh continued as he took hold of my arm and in a hushed voice he asked.

'Do you believe in miracles?'

He caught me quite off guard with this unusual question.

'Well, I don't k...know, never thought about it really,' I stammered awkwardly.

'Mm, yes, funny sort of thing for me to ask wouldn't you say?'

'Yes, well I had better go now,' I said hurriedly wishing to get away.

'Thank you for these.'

'You are very welcome my boy,' and as he made his way back to his shop I noticed that his gaze never left the man, not once.

Mr Singh's question had quite unnerved me as I had been thinking along those same lines myself and as I approached the man he gave me a long look.

'Anything wrong,' he asked.

'No, nothing. Mr. Singh just gave me some of his son's old clothes that's all.'

'That was good of him.'

'Mm,' I nodded.

'Did you enjoy the run?'

'Oh yes, it was marvellous, can't remember the last time I felt so alive.'

'Gets the blood pumping and also gives you an appetite so let's head for the bakers and see if we fancy anything to eat in there.'

'Fine with me.'

And then I thought I would broach the subject of Mr. Singh's back.

'He seemed a lot better.'

'Who,' he asked absentmindedly as he strode along his mind obviously elsewhere.

'Mr. Singh, his painful back, remember.'

'Oh yes.'

'It's much better now.'
'Mm hm.'
Did you... did you have anything to do with that?'
'With what?'
'Mr. Singh's back,' I was getting annoyed now as he surely wasn't listening to me.
'Why would you ask that of me?'
'Well, he asked me if I believed in miracles and he gave me the impression he thought you had healed him of his back pain.'
And then turning towards me he asked if I believed that.
'I don't know, maybe,' and he smiled that enigmatic smile of his.
'Let's go this way Mike, someone needs our help,' and he headed off leaving me with so many unanswered questions.

15

An Old Seafarer

As we made our way towards the bakers I became aware that he seemed quite concerned about an elderly man half-lying on one of the benches provided for people to take their ease.

And as I started to take an interest as well I watched horrified as the old chap began to slide over as if he had lost his balance or was unwell.

The man, as I knew he would, rushed to his side and checked to see what was wrong.

Anyone could see he was in a bad way - his hair was unkempt, he looked as if he hadn't shaved in days and his clothes were dirty and worn.

'What has happened my friend,' he asked, placing a comforting arm around his shoulders.

His hands were blue with cold and I don't think I would have been wrong in thinking that he might have hyperthermia.

I wondered aloud how long he might have been sitting there.

'I saw him on our way up to the big house,' the man answered.

And to my shame I hadn't even noticed him.

'Mike, run up to the cafe and buy a hot drink for this poor fellow and maybe a sandwich or two, here is some money,' and he pressed the money the woman had given him into my hand.

Just as I was about to do as requested I watched him remove his jacket and place it over the old gent, and so I did likewise.

'Mike you don't have to do that.'

'It's ok, I'm glad to help out,' I retorted slightly annoyed he was treating me like a kid.

'Very well then, but hurry.'

And I sped off.

I quickly returned laden down with a small thermos of hot chocolate and a large bag containing various meats and bread.

'Did I give you enough money for all that,' he asked in surprise, eyeing everything I had brought back.

'The cook gave me all this for free when I explained about the man.'

'That was generous of her, it's the little things that make a difference Mike, every time.'

Then turning towards the old man he beckoned me over to introduce us.

'Mike, this is Tom Wilson, an old sea dog who fought in the navy during the second world war.'

'Tom, this is Mike.'

The old man seemed thoroughly bemused by what was going on but managed to nod in my direction anyway.

'Let's get some food and drink into this seafarer before he faints again.'

'I don't want anything,' he said, pushing my hand holding the cup away from him.

So the man went and stood squarely in front of him saying, 'we're here to help you Tom, not going to let you give up.'

'Too late for that,' he grumbled.

'All my ol' pals have gone, the wife died years ago and the kids...' and here he gave a heart-rending sigh before continuing.

'They've flown the nest and gone their separate ways, and now I rarely see them '

'Just leave me be, please.'

'Not going to do that old-timer, now come on, just take a sip of this and I promise you will start to feel better once you're warm,' and the man proceeded to hold the cup to his lips exactly as he had done to me.

'Tom, drink please, it's delicious,' I begged, overcome with sadness for this elderly man who had no one.

And so he did, slowly at first, and then he downed the whole lot and even smacked his lips as he finished.

'You're right son - that were real nice, thank you.'

'Where do you live Tom,' the man asked.

'We will take you home.'

'Over there,' he indicated with a dirty finger.

'On top of the bread shop.'

'Well that's good, we were on our way there anyway so we can accompany you.'

'Let's get you up Tom,' and he took hold of one arm and I took the other.

He almost seemed to creak as he stood up.

'My old bones,' he grimaced.

We helped him across the road to the passageway where the bakers was situated and as we reached his front door he shook our hands off, thanked us, and said that he was perfectly alright now.

'Are you sure,' the man queried.

'Yes, I'm sure,' and he rummaged around in a pocket in search of his key.

Retrieving it he then had trouble finding the lock so the man gently took it from him and opened the door.

Once inside he took back his key, grabbed hold of the bag of food and drink that I held out to him and promptly shut the door in our faces.

'Well, I like that, wasn't very grateful was he.'

'Life has handed him a raw deal so can you really blame him.'

'I suppose not.'

'Let's get some lunch then,' and he steered me away towards the bakers.

On our way back to the cottage after buying a couple of pies I noticed the man in deep thought.

'What's up,' I asked.

'Can't be easy can it, getting old and lonely.'

'I guess not, it's bad enough when you're young - being lonely I mean.'

He nodded his wise head in total agreement.

16

A Living Being

Just as we were passing by a narrow alleyway I was alerted to the sound of excited children's voices.

I could see the man was interested as well at all the commotion.

'What's going on do you think,' I asked.

'Well, there's only one way to find out,' and off he went with a determined air about him.

'Here we go again, never a dull moment with you around,' I muttered but I was secretly pleased at having such an enquiring companion.

But then he started to run and called out to them.

'Stop right there!

Wait!'

However, there was no way they were going to hang around with a seemingly cross adult bearing down on them.

If only they knew what he was really like I thought, sad they probably never would.

As I ran after him, at a total loss as to what was going on, I heard their raised voices calling out obscenities that were almost beyond belief out of the mouths of just seven and eight year olds.

When I finally caught up with him I could see that he was almost beside himself as he reached down and tenderly picked something up off the ground and held it close into his body as if to shield it.

The children, by now had scattered but I could still hear their raucous, laughing voices fading away into the distance as they scarpered.

'What is it?'

'It's a cat, they were throwing stones at it, look see, it's barely alive.'

'How could young children behave like that to such a poor little thing,' I asked.

As I took in the small, bloodied ball of what looked like just grey fluff, and then to hear it give a pitiful miaow, my anger knew no bounds.

'It's still alive, I can't believe it.'

'Believe it,' he said, having calmed down.

I rounded on him then so I could vent my own feelings of disgust.

'I bet you never get angry do you,' and his back stiffened at my words and as he turned towards me I saw his jaw tighten.

'You would lose your bet,' he said simply, and as he walked away from me I saw him surreptitiously wipe away a tear.

So much for my thinking he didn't care.

'How can little kids be so cruel,' I yelled after him, still angry.

Then halting in mid-stride he answered,

'Children are the personification of innocence, until they learn the ways of the world.'

And as he stroked the tiny creature, to my astonishment, it actually began to purr.

'Well, would you listen to that,' I exclaimed.

'Come on little thing,' the man said.

'Let's take you to your new home,' and off he marched, so fast I could hardly keep up.

'Where are we taking it?'

'Toms',' came the decided reply.

'What,' I exploded

'He can't even look after himself let alone a half dead cat.'
'It will give him a reason to keep living and not to give up.'

As we made our way back to where Tom lived I happened to notice Benny watching us with a curious look on his face; and then I recalled that I'd also seen him when Mr. Singh had stopped me, and then thinking about it, he had been there in the crowd listening to the elderly woman who had been on that stricken coach as well.

I felt almost as if he were stalking me, weird thing for a fellow like him to do.

Oh well, if it pleases him to follow me around as long as he keeps his distance that was fine by me.

'But what do I do with it,' Tom growled when he opened his front door and the man explained what he wanted.

'Feed it and love it, the same as for every living being,' and I saw the old man's face soften as he asked:

'Is that what you did for me?'

Then after sighing heavily, he reluctantly said he would, 'one good turn deserves another I suppose.'

'I'd better get some old newspapers you can put it on - it's a right mess and no mistake,' and he scurried off back inside.

'Pah!'

Ugh, it's filthy,' he groused unhappily as he took hold of the small animal.

'Please, don't do me any more favours,' he directed at us.

'I can't be takin' in all the waifs and strays now can I,' and with that he shut and bolted his door, but at least he didn't slam it.

'Do you think he will take care of it,' I asked worriedly as we walked away.

'I'm certain of it.'

'How can you be so sure?'

'He's a seaman, sailors and cats go hand in hand.'

'Do they?'

'Uh huh.'

' Well I've never heard that before.'

'Neither have I, but there's always a first time isn't there,' and he chucked me under the chin laughing at the look I gave him, and it was a relief to see him happy again.

17

A Story

The days went by so fast now and inevitably the weather became warmer and one fine sunny day the man suggested we have our lunch down on the beach.

Having made a couple of sandwiches and grabbed a bottle of water we then made our way down to the water's edge and sat down.

The sun was shining brightly and I found myself cloaked in a feeling of such happiness as I sat beside my dearest friend in all the world.

Feeling totally at ease we tossed pebbles into the sea where they made a delightful plopping sound.

As the sun climbed higher into the cloudless blue sky we decided the time was about right to have lunch; besides I was famished even though I had eaten a hearty breakfast.

Along with the bracing sea air and the good company I was keeping I found that I had developed quite an appetite these days.

There weren't many people alongside us so we almost had the beach to ourselves so it was quite surprising when all of a sudden a large group of children appeared.

The man, (I still couldn't bring myself to refer to him as Jesus) made them all sit down in front of us in a semicircle.

I wondered vaguely where they had all come from as there weren't that many other adults around apart from us that I could see.

We had been in the process of eating our sandwiches when I realised they were eyeing our food hungrily.

I looked at him and he returned the look and so without either of us saying a word we began to divide the bread up to give to them.

After we had distributed the small meal they munched away quite happily.

When they had eaten their fill and were fully sated one little girl near the front stood up, and shyly asked if she could maybe sit on the man's lap.

Without a second thought and looking really pleased at this request he manoeuvred himself onto a nearby rock and picking her up she snuggled down contentedly sucking her thumb.

She was about three years old and a sweet little thing with curly brown hair and pink cheeks.

As I watched these proceedings I suddenly had a vision of what it must have been like all those years ago.

If he was who he said he was his clothing would have been different but I could imagine him loving and blessing the children around him as he was doing right now.

Then one bright little chap with ginger hair and a snub nose leapt to his feet and called for a story, and then a chorus of shrill voices echoed his.

'Very well then,' and the man settled back comfortably, happy to oblige.

'Once upon a time there was a little girl...' and his gaze immediately fell onto the child he was holding, 'and she lived in an orphanage as both her parents had died. She was a very unhappy child, she never smiled or laughed and her mouth was always turned down miserably. She neither ate nor drank very much and so she lost a lot of weight, she wasn't very big to start with and so the workers at the orphanage became very concerned for her wellbeing. They took her aside and asked her to tell them what was wrong as they treated her exactly the same as the other children and they appeared to be fairly ok, but she just stared at them mutely, her eyes giving nothing away.

Eventually they became so worried they decided she should see a doctor, but he just gave her some pills to take and said she would probably grow out of it.

The pills had no effect whatsoever and so they then took her to see a priest who did a lot of talking and read something from a book.

All to no avail.

The workers were in despair as she was getting thinner and weaker by the day. Then someone thought that maybe a trip away from the orphanage might help.

So they rounded up all the children onto a coach ready for a day's outing in London to see the sights.

Unfortunately the little girl by now had become so weak they almost had to carry her everywhere.

Nothing was of any interest to her until by chance as they walked along the road they spotted a young man singing and playing a guitar - he was a busker.

They came to a halt beside him to listen to the song he was currently singing. It was a slow, wistful lullaby and his warm velvety voice drew them all into a place where there was no more hurt and no more pain.

Complete silence fell over them as the last strains of the song died away, and then they all burst into loud applause and onlookers tipped change into his guitar case as a reward for such a beautiful song.

Maybe the sound of the young man's voice called to the little girl I don't know but all at once she tiptoed over to stand meekly before him.

She looked so pitiful that the young man immediately lay down his guitar, patted his knee and suggested that she might like to sit there.

Unexpectedly, she nodded.

He was a kind young man, he didn't make much money busking but he was happy as long as he could make music.

Saddened by the sorry look on her downcast face he threw his arms around her and hugged her like she had never been hugged before.

The workers at the orphanage did their best but they didn't have the time or the energy to go around cuddling all the children in their care.

Eventually, he pulled away from her and as he did so tears as big as raindrops started to well up in her big blue eyes and run like rivulets down her pale cheeks.

The workers had never known her to cry before so this was really unusual.

And as they fell the young musician collected them and as if by magic they turned to pearls in his hand.

Ever so slowly a small smile creased her face and unexpectedly she began to laugh and he, so pleased to see this amazing change in her, laughed as well'.

At this point I remembered what the man had said to me when I was threatening to jump off that cliff and so end my life:

Tears are meant to be shed, not bottled up inside where they can cause such a lot of pain.

'The workers, some with tears in their eyes, gradually moved off ushering their small charges before them.

Seeing they were walking away now the young man placed the little girl gently back on the ground and said that she had better follow them.

As she turned away she gave a skip and then a jump and she even started humming to herself; and as he watched fascinated at this remarkable transformation she did a little dance along the street and when she abruptly came to a halt and turned to gaze lovingly back at him, she raised a hand to her lips and blew him a kiss which he caught and placed firmly onto his cheek.

And for the rest of that day as he sang and played his guitar passers-by couldn't help but notice the faint but beautiful outline of a butterfly on his cheek.

As for the little girl, she started to thrive now eating and drinking heartily.

No longer was she thin and withdrawn with no interest in anything.

She laughed and played with the other children and it was as if a huge weight had been lifted from her shoulders.

She was happy'.

As the crowd of children melted away now that the story was finished I noticed the small girl still on the man's lap and she seemed quite content to stay where she was.

Eventually though he placed her gently back on the ground and told her to join the others.

She looked up at him with such love on her face, her eyes as big as saucers and then she gave a little giggle, waved goodbye, and was gone.

'Come on then,' he said, getting to his feet, 'we can't sit here idly all day.'

As we walked back across the now empty beach it dawned on me that we had taken only a handful of sandwiches with us and from them we had fed around thirty youngsters.

And as if reading my thoughts, he turned looked straight at me, and putting his arm around my shoulders said:

'Never underestimate the power of love Mike, its effect is truly amazing as you yourself have just witnessed.'

18

A Boy

After the episode on the beach with the children and the small amount of food that curiously had fed them all I thought he could never again faze me with anything else he did.

How wrong could I have been?

We were in town one morning as the man needed to replace some tools for his carpentry.

Having purchased the items he wanted from a hardware store we had just finished a late lunch and were on our way back to the bus stop when we came upon a horde of Secondary School pupils streaming out from a side road.

Many of them appeared to be in shock and several girls were crying and holding fast to one another for comfort.

The man, as expected, hurried off down the street to see what was occurring.

As we approached a small huddled group appeared to be at a bit of a loss.

And then we saw the figure of a boy lying on the ground writhing in agony with pain etched all over his young face.

He had been stabbed and the handle of the knife could clearly be seen as he gripped it with blood dripping from the wound onto his hands.

Nobody seemed to be doing anything to help him, the kids milling around just looked shell-shocked and transfixed with horror.

Realising somebody had to do something and quickly I nudged one of the boys and suggested he run to the nearest phone box and call for an ambulance.

At first he ignored me so I grabbed hold of his shoulders and shook him to bring him to his senses, and then he tore off down the street almost tripping over in his haste.

As I looked back to see how the boy was doing I was aghast to notice that he had now stopped writhing and was completely still and as I watched dumbfounded his eyes glazed over.

He was dying there right in front of me on that dirty, rubbish strewn street alone and in agony.

Time seemed to stand still, nobody moved, nobody spoke - we were stunned at what had just happened.

Then, as if in slow motion, the man walked silently over to where the youngster lay and kneeling down beside him put his hands one on top of the other on the open wound and pressed down firmly after first removing the knife.

It's a bit late for that now I thought, he's almost certainly gone.

Knowing him as I was starting to, I knew he would be devastated at this senseless loss of life.

Going over to where he was kneeling I touched him lightly on the shoulder saying, 'I think it's too late to save him, I'm sorry but I think he's gone.'

Ignoring me, I heard him utter a few soft words and immediately I was amazed to see the boy's eyes flicker open and to hear him take a shuddering breath.

Rising to his feet he gave the now bemused boy a long look and then prepared to make his way back through the crowd of pupils that had now gathered around him chattering excitedly.

Ambulance men and a police officer were hurrying down the road towards us, almost knocking me over in their haste.

The man looked tired as if all the energy had drained out of him so taking hold of his arm I helped him walk away from the horde of people that had now come to see what was going on.

As we made our escape a man's voice could clearly be heard saying, 'well, I don't understand it at all, there's a lot of blood in fact the kid's covered in it, but where's the wound?'

I wondered vaguely what he was talking about, anyone could see the boy had been stabbed almost to the point of death, and the man had tried to stem the bleeding with his hands and I had seen the boy's eyes open and heard him take a breath.

What did he mean when he asked where was the wound? We all saw it.

Trying to get my head around all that had happened it gradually started to sink in that maybe, just maybe, the man had brought him back from the brink.

In fact, asking him to wait a moment I then hurried back to the scene and was shocked to see the boy standing up unaided as if nothing had happened and the ambulance men looking quite rightly annoyed to have been called out on a wasted trip.

I was gobsmacked!

Returning to where I had left the man I found him sitting on the kerbside waiting for me.

He looked pale but pleased to see me.

'Ready,' he asked.

'Shall we go?'

'Sure,' I replied, not trusting myself to say anything further.

Then as we started to walk away he made a sudden grab for my arm.

'Wait a second.'

He had noticed something lying on the ground where I had been just about to place my foot.

There was a worm, looking slightly the worse for wear, if it stayed where it was any longer it would almost certainly get trodden on.

I watched fascinated as he bent down, and gently placing it in his hand, lowered the small creature into someone's front garden where it would now be safe from flying feet.

'It's easy to kill Mike, even by accident; all life is precious,' he reminded me.

Even a little worm.

19

The Storm

I awoke one morning to the sound of distant rumbling and going over to the window and drawing back the curtains I saw that the sky looked dark and angry; and as I stood there a clap of thunder that seemed to make the very earth shake made me leap back in fright and so I was very relieved to escape to the silence of the kitchen away from the crashing noises that chilled me to the bone.

After the man appeared we drank hot cups of tea and buttered toast in silence listening to the noise the storm was making all too aware that it was edging its way ever closer towards us.

I put on the light to brighten the gloom of the day and then cleared the table of the now empty cups and plates.

When I returned from the kitchen I went and sat in one of the big old armchairs to read a magazine I had come across recently to keep myself occupied while the man repaired a chest of drawers.

And all the while the encroaching storm was gathering momentum out at sea.

The man had buried himself in his work but every so now and again he would peer over towards the window with a frown creasing his forehead.

'Fair old storm coming our way,' I remarked casually.

'You're not wrong there Mike, a real humdinger this one.'

'I wouldn't like to be caught out at sea in this, quite frightening I should think,' I said as I put down my magazine and went to stand by the window to look out.

The wind had risen dramatically now and the rolling waves were coming hurtling onto the beach below us sending spray ten feet or more high into the air.

The thunderous sounds it was making had grown in intensity and it was as if it was almost right on top of us.

And then I saw it.

A boat in the distance struggled valiantly against the might of this monster storm and it was being tossed about like a toy in a bathtub that a child would play with but this was no toy and from what I could gather there were many people on board, in fact it looked almost like a rescue boat.

'Oh boy, I wouldn't like to be on that,' I muttered.

'On what,' the man asked as he joined me at the window.

Then, without saying a word, and flinging the door open wide he rushed from the room, and I watched in horror, my heart in my mouth, as he ran down to the water's edge.

I couldn't imagine what he thought he could do, he would never be able to swim out to that heaving boat and even if he did, which I doubted, the storm was so fierce one man alone would be useless against its ferocity.

But then, as I was starting to realise, *He* was no ordinary man.

However, I couldn't bear to think about what would happen if even He was no match for this horrendous storm.

Coming away from the window I went and sat down again, there was nothing I could do, but I couldn't relax knowing that he was out there somewhere battling the wind and the enormous waves.

After a while, and he still hadn't returned I forced myself back to the window and couldn't quite believe what was unfolding before me.

The boat was still floundering and the storm hadn't abated even a little in fact it seemed to have become stronger and louder.

And then I saw him.

He was out there quite close to the rolling boat, and he appeared to be standing on the water.

I couldn't believe what I was seeing, in fact I had to look away and rub my eyes, such was my astonishment.

When I could bring myself to look again I had to shake my head in disbelief.

As I watched dumbfounded I saw him slowly raise his arms skyward and then, as he lowered them, the thunder quietened, the wind dropped and the sea became as still and flat as a millpond.

The boat then scurried hurriedly back towards the shore with some very relieved passengers on board.

And then he disappeared.

If I hadn't seen that with my own eyes I would never have believed it, and I remembered then what that elderly woman from the coach had said.

She wouldn't have believed it possible, and now I felt the same way.

Going back to my chair I waited impatiently for him to return and when a few minutes later he walked through the door as calm as you like, his face radiant and dry as a bone I couldn't help but marvel, and had to admit finally that he really was who he said he was.

'I saw you,' I said, my voice a strangled whisper and I had to cough to try and regain some control over myself.

'I saw you, out there on the sea,' I tried again.

'Oh yes,' he said simply.

And his eyes twinkled merrily at me.

'Just another day at the office Mike, just another day.'

'Let's have something to eat,' he said, eyeing me warily, 'then I have a job of work to do in town.'

'Ok fine,' I croaked.

'Something wrong with your voice,' he asked innocently knowing full well I was shaken by what I had seen him do.

I shook my head not trusting myself to say anything further.

20

A Prostitute

We had a small meal of bread and cheese and the man made some hot chocolate.

'Are you happy to come with me,' he asked as we cleared the table, 'or would you prefer to stay here, you look a little pale.

Are you feeling alright?'

'I'm ok thanks, and yes I would like to come.'

My voice luckily had returned to normal but I still felt as if I'd just been hit with a sledgehammer.

'Well, alright then, I'll get my tools together and then we'll go,' and I could tell by the concerned look he gave me that he was very aware he had shocked me.

We took the bus and it took us quite a while to get to our destination as roadworks held us up but eventually we arrived and the man made ready to work on a very large cabinet that I could tell would take up most of the afternoon.

So I decided to go for a walk while he worked to try and get my head around what I had seen him do earlier.

When he had previously told me who he was I obviously hadn't believed him.

Besides it was all too ridiculous for words, but after everything I had been party to recently I had begun to wonder.

And after this morning's episode I now had no doubt at all that he was who he said he was and that, I had to admit, was pretty startling.

The work on the cabinet took a whole lot longer than I had anticipated and it was well into the evening before we could at last take our leave.

Retracing our journey seemed to go on for ever as we encountered so much traffic on a go-slow past the road works again but eventually we arrived back at the bus stop at the top of the hill.

We were now both tired and hungry so as we passed by the Cockleshell Inn we saw that it was still serving customers so we decided to go inside for a very welcome meal and drink.

After we were well fed and watered and now very eager to get home the man paid the bill and after exchanging pleasantries with the barman we left.

While I waited for the man to join me outside I was surprised to see a woman of the streets leaning casually up against the wall of the pub.

I knew immediately what she was as her whole demeanour shouted sex for sale.

With a cigarette dangling from one hand and eyeing the man up and down as he came out she then sauntered casually across to us with a leery grin plastered across her face.

I had only ever seen prostitutes when I roamed the streets of London and didn't think for one moment that I would come across one down here in this lowly seaside village.

I wondered vaguely if she ever managed to do any business around here but then I came to the conclusion that tonight probably was a one off as maybe she couldn't be bothered to venture further afield.

'Hello handsome,' she said, coming to a halt immediately in front of him.

'How about it then, fancy a bit o' fun?'

'Don't cost a lot, I'm cheap, don't yer know,' she said, running the tip of her tongue seductively across her heavily painted mouth.

She wasn't a young woman by any means and as her short skirt had risen up sharply as she moved revealing naked white flesh I felt my skin crawl.

Realising who she was coming on to upset me more than I can say but he didn't appear to be at all perturbed by her drunken swaying advances, if anything his face had taken on a look of great sadness that I wasn't at all prepared for.

I thought he should have been disgusted at her blatant lack of propriety but I couldn't have been more wrong.

After glancing quickly over at me, she then shocked me by saying that maybe we could have a threesome.

The breath caught in my throat at such an unthinkable idea and I involuntarily recoiled in horror at what she was suggesting.

The whole time she had been speaking she had avoided the man's face but then she made the mistake of looking up and straight into his eyes.

Her mouth began to tremble and her face crumpled and then as a loud sob tore itself from her throat she turned and fled as fast as her shabby high heels would allow her.

I knew at once what had happened.

The man had an aura of goodness about him and when she had looked into his eyes and seen herself reflected there she hadn't liked what she'd seen and so she had run from him, or more likely herself.

And a moment before she raced off I happened to notice the man reach out a hand as if to comfort her but all to no avail; she was gone and he astonishingly looked stricken that he hadn't been able to help her.

I should have known by now that was his way, and instead of being appalled as I had been, his reaction straightaway had been to show her compassion.

'Some people, including myself, have a sickness inside them,' I heard myself saying.

'And no matter how hard they try to overcome it they usually find it's impossible.

And then wanting to know more about what it had been like for him nearly two thousand years ago.

'I bet you weren't afraid when they came for you, you know - the soldiers.

I mean after all, you are the Son of God,' I remarked flippantly.

'Well, again you would lose your bet, I was very afraid. My spirit was willing, but the flesh is weak.'

'Why did you have to die,' I asked suitably chastised.

'It was necessary, unless a grain of wheat falls to the ground and dies it remains alone, but only if it dies will it bear fruit.'

'That seems rather harsh.'

'Yes, but it had to be.

Sheep tend to run amok if left unattended, and so it is with people.'

'And you are the shepherd.'

Now I understood.

'Yes, if only people would listen to me,' and there was a note of sadness in his voice.

'I wasn't listening.'

'No.'

'But I am now.'

And I watched his spirits visibly lift.

'Was...was it very painful?'

Words were not necessary as a cloud passed over his face and I watched him shudder violently at the memory.

Feeling all at once very small and insignificant beside the magnificence of this man and wanting somehow to show my gratitude I reached across and laid a hand on his shoulder and the tortured look he gave me shook me to the core.

22

Elizabeth

One morning very early before it was even light there came a frantic hammering on the cottage door.

Still groggy from sleep I somehow stumbled across the floor to answer it and you could have knocked me over with a feather when I recognised the boy standing there.

It was none other than our 'shadow' who had been following me around for the past few weeks - Benny.

Pushing past me he barged his way inside and demanded to see the man.

'Hey, wait a minute you can't come...' but the fierce look on his face suggested I keep quiet and do as he asked.

'I'll go and fetch him then,' and just as I turned away the man came strolling into the room half-dressed, hair tousled and rubbing his eyes.

'What's going on?' he asked, stifling a yawn.

Benny walked straight up to him and grabbed hold of his clothing.

'You've got to come with me...now.'

'Oh yes, and why is that?'

'Do you know what time it is,' I interjected.

'I know exactly what the time is, and you can mind your own business,' he snapped angrily at me.

Anyone could see that even though he was being thoroughly boorish he was also quite distraught.

'My mother is critically ill in hospital, she has stomach cancer...and she's dying. We almost lost her last night but they managed to revive her, but next time...' and here his voice trailed away.

'You must come,' he said, taking hold of the man's arm, 'there's no time to lose.'

Finally extricating himself from Benny's vice-like grip he asked why it should be he who should go to his mother's aid.

'I've seen and heard things about you, weird things, and I don't know if any of it is true, but there is nobody else,' he stressed.

'Now, will you come,' he was almost begging now.

'Yes, of course I'll come, but let me get dressed properly first though.'

'Ok, but hurry... please,' he added grudgingly and he instantly began to prowl around the room like a caged animal.

'Be alright if I come too,' I asked quietly, not wanting to add to his agitation.

'If you must.'

He lit a cigarette then with hands that shook and puffed away furiously.

'You don't mind,' he asked, indicating the smoke, daring me to say otherwise.

'No, of course not,' and shaking my head I surprised myself by actually starting to feel sorry for him.

'How far is the hospital where your mother is,' the man asked when he reappeared.

'She's no longer in the cottage hospital, when she worsened she was moved to the big one in town about five miles away.'

After the man shut the front door with a bang Benny rushed off ahead of us calling over his shoulder that the bus would be leaving soon so we had better hurry.

It was chilly that morning but luckily dry underfoot which enabled the three of us to race up the hill to where the bus was stationary.

Fortunately the conductor had seen us coming and bade the driver wait.

The man thanked him for keeping the bus back and I marvelled at how nice he always was.

'No problem,' and the conductor grinning, cheerfully saluted.

The journey didn't take long and as soon as we arrived Benny led the way inside having first discarded his third cigarette.

It was still quite dark and as we walked in silence along the corridor the lights illuminating the walls with a greenish glow made me feel quite nauseous and I wondered how anyone could ever get better in a place like this.

We passed ward after ward full to the brim with long lines of patients and then out of this depressing atmosphere I heard the man give a great sigh.

'So many sick people,' and his face took on a dark haunted look, and I realised then how much it must hurt him to witness so much suffering.

Eventually Benny came to a halt outside a side room just off the main corridor.

'She's in there,' and he gestured with his arm seemingly reluctant to go inside.

'What is her name?'

'Elizabeth.'

The man stepping forward entered the room and I followed at a safe distance not wanting to get in the way.

Benny's mother lay prone on the bed still and white-faced and for a horrible moment I thought we were too late but then I heard her give a little moan.

Going over to the bed where she lay the man knelt down on the floor beside her, and reaching out gently, took hold of her hand.

'Hello Elizabeth.'

There was no response, not surprising really if she was as bad as Benny had made out, no wonder he had been in such a state and even though he had treated us badly he obviously loved his mother, and rightly so.

And then turning towards me he said, 'let's go Mike.'

'I'll see you again won't I,' he called after us.

'As long as you don't knock us down,' the man replied, giving me a quick wink.

'Oh I won't, I promise you.'

He was falling over his words in his excitement and willingness to apologise.

'Well, you sure made his day,' I announced as we walked away, 'and his mother's too of course,' I added.

'It's good to make anyone's day, wouldn't you agree?'

And I had to admit it was.

23

Holly

As we attempted to make our way back through the maze of corridors inevitably we became quite lost.

'Where is the exit,' I asked exasperatedly, wanting to leave as soon as possible as hospitals always gave me the creeps.

We passed ward after ward of occupied beds until eventually we came across the children's ward and here the man stopped abruptly to peer inside.

Pushing aside the closed doors he crossed the threshold and made his way over to the nearest bed.

Sitting on the edge of it and looking quite glum sat a tiny girl.

She was the prettiest little thing with a smattering of freckles across a dainty nose and rosebud lips that trembled slightly at the sight of us.

With her hands clasped in front of her as if in prayer she reminded me of an angel such was her countenance.

The man sat down on the chair by her bedside, and I crept quietly after him wondering what he intended to do this time.

'Hello,' he spoke gently, not wishing to scare her.
'Hello Mister,' she replied.
'Are you a doctor?'
'No, I'm not a doctor.'
,'Oh, I'm glad,' and a look of relief swept across her face. 'I was afraid you might want to give me something horrible to drink,' and she wrinkled her nose in disgust.
'What's your name?'

When he returned to Holly's bedside, and after touching her cheek tenderly, he promised that she would get better soon.

Gazing up at him almost in awe she asked him what his name was.

'It's Jesus, have you heard of me?'

When she shook her head he seemed very downcast.

As we got up to leave and she gave a little wave regretfully, we both waved back simultaneously.

'What a beautiful child,' I uttered as we pushed our way out through the confining doors to the corridor.

'Shame she is so sick.'

'She won't be for long,' and raising his hand to touch the frame of the door he then bowed his head against it.

I knew this stance so well.

'Let's go home,' he said, pulling himself away but not before peering back through the window for a last look at Holly.

In a few days time the local newspapers had a field day as all their headlines were of, 'The Miracle Children.'

That whole ward of children were all home now after unexpectedly all being healed of their illnesses.

All on the same day.

24

Rita

That night around ten o'clock there came a quiet tapping on the front door, and when the man went to open it there stood the hunched figure of the prostitute we had seen only a few days previously and this time she was an even sorrier sight than before.

Her clothes were torn, she had a black eye where someone had obviously smashed a fist into it, her scarlet lipstick was smeared across her mouth in an ugly mess and she was shaking from head to foot and appeared to be finding it very difficult to stand still.

The man guided her inside and helped her to sit in his now vacant chair and throwing a blanket that he always kept there around her he then knelt down beside the almost incoherent woman.

'What has happened,' he questioned gently, taking her bloodied face in his hand and stroking it softly with his thumb.

She looked round at him and straightaway huge tears began to cascade down her cheeks and she brushed them away with the back of a grubby hand.

'I'll go and make a hot drink for her,' I said, feeling that I should give her some space to collect herself.

'Good idea Mike,' and at his words she lowered her eyes to stare at the floor overcome with shame as she recalled our last meeting.

As I busied myself making the hot chocolate I could hear them speaking together in low voices.

When I returned with the drink I saw that he was holding both her hands in his and he was listening attentively to everything she was saying.

Evidently it would seem that the 'client' she'd had earlier that evening refused to pay up and he had then beaten her to within an inch of her life.

'We must report this to the police,' he was insisting, 'he could very likely do this again to some other unfortunate woman.'

'No, I can't do that,' she said, frowning at the very idea of going to the police.

'Well then Rita, you know what you must do even before I say it don't you.'

'Yes,' she whispered meekly.

'Give it up?'

'Yes.'

He had that concerned look on his face again, one that I have seen so often and then he announced that he would get a cold cloth for her face and getting to his feet disappeared into the kitchen.

'To be honest,' she said, turning towards me, 'I was a little afraid of coming here wondering what he would do and say...but there was nobody else.'

I felt for her then, she was completely alone in the world and so was I, but at least I had the man I thought smugly.

Little did I know that we would soon be parting, and I would be devastated.

She drank the hot chocolate I brought her, thanked me and then apologised profusely.

'I'm sorry about... you know, the other day when you came across me outside the pub.'

Gone was the brash attitude and language and she now sounded quite pleasant.

'That's alright,' I said.

'I was rude, and it was unforgivable.'

'He will forgive you if you ask him.'

' Will he,' she seemed unsure.

'He's so kind isn't he,' and she started to cry again.

'Yes he is, remarkably so.'

Returning with the cold cloth he looked at Rita and then at me with a questioning look on his face.

'It's alright, we were talking about you not to you,' I said cheekily.

'Well, I hope it was something nice.'

'It was,' Rita said, 'very, very nice.'

'Well, I think we could all do with some rest now, especially you Rita. You can take my bed and I will sleep in the chair, and no arguments,' when he saw she was about to protest.

'She could always take my bed,' I piped up but he wouldn't hear of it.

'Maybe I should just go back,' she whispered, obviously not wanting to be a nuisance.

'No, you can stay here until you feel a little stronger,' and taking her by the hand showed her where she could wash up and where his bedroom was.

'I will never be able to repay you.'

'You can, by giving up the life you've been leading.'

'I will, I promise,' I heard her say as she shut the bedroom door.

And I hoped she really would, realising what a challenge she faced.

What a difference there was between the fine clothes and icy coldness of this clergyman and of the shabby, well-worn clothing the man wore and of his warm kindness.

'*You*, it would appear have been using sorcery of the worst kind,' he continued.

'Are you a devil-worshipper?'

'Hardly.'

'Well, he wouldn't, considering he's the...'

The man signalled to me to be quiet here, and I realised that I should probably keep my mouth shut about who he was and then he said the words that would floor me.

'Well, I am sure you will be very relieved to hear that I will be leaving the area very shortly so I will no longer be a problem for you.'

I never knew that someone could smile with their mouth but not with their eyes.

I did now.

'Well, I'm very glad to hear it,' the bishop said, rising from his chair and making his way over to the front door eager to get away.

'I hope we will not see the likes of you again.'

'You won't,' and closing the door behind him I heard the man release his breath as if he had been holding it all in.

'What a horrible man,' Rita uttered.

'Father forgive me,' I heard the man say.

And I, momentarily forgetting he may be divine but that he had human emotions as well.

'What did you mean when you said you would soon be leaving,' I asked tightly as my mouth had suddenly gone dry.

'Just that Mike, it's time for me to go and for you to go back to your life.'

'What life, my life is here now with you, there's nothing for me without you.'

'There's no need to be afraid Mike, for I will always be with you.'

26

The Long Goodbye

It had started out as a dismal rainy day, but after the bishop left the skies cleared and the sunshine beckoned.

'What say you two we go for a walk and then maybe go for some lunch,' the man asked.

He was being perfectly pleasant as usual but I could tell the bishop's visit had unsettled him.

Rita was only too pleased to get out into the fresh air but I was feeling hurt and upset that the man was leaving and I would be alone again, even though he had said he would always be with me, but I didn't understand what he meant by that.

How could he still be with me?

It was starting to turn into what promised to be a gloriously warm day and the man after placing an arm around both of us as we walked commented on how happy he was to be out and about with his friends, but I noticed that his eyes looked sad.

Rita, looking up at him smiled and thanked him for that, but I stayed silent.

After a while we became aware of somebody trotting hurriedly up behind us and as we slowed to a halt and looked to see who was there Tom the old seaman appeared beaming from ear to ear.

'I'm so glad to see you again,' he puffed after the exertion of the steep walk uphill.

'I so wanted to thank you for giving me Silver.'

The man, frowning, replied that he hadn't given him any...

'No, you don't understand,' he said laughing.

'Look,' and reaching a hand inside his jacket he then produced this amazingly beautiful silvery grey coloured tabby cat.

'Silver I named her, quite obvious really wouldn't you say,' he chuckled.

'Oh my,' the man exclaimed.

'I had thought she might not survive as she was so hurt, but just look at her now,' and the man tickled the little animal behind the ears and she looked up at him adoringly.

'She has turned my life around you know, and it's all thanks to you,' and there were tears in his eyes as he pumped first the man's hand and then mine.

'I'm so happy for you Tom,' the man said 'and you are to be congratulated for taking such good care of her.'

'Well, goodbye for now,' he said, suddenly overcome with emotion and he hurried off sniffing and wiping his nose.

'Have to go and feed her,' he called over his shoulder and with a quick wave he dashed off with the energy of a man half his age back down the hill towards his rooms.

'Well, that's a better start to the day,' the man muttered clearly pleased.

Eventually we came upon the old inn and Rita said regretfully that she needed to go home now, and after thanking us for everything we had done for her we watched her walk away.

She looked small and vulnerable and I felt quite worried as I knew how hard it would be for her to turn her life around without help.

'Do you think she will actually stop,' I queried.

'We can only hope, but I'm sure she will give it her best shot, after all not very pleasant being beaten up.'

As we made our way through the village we had to keep stopping as some of the villagers who had come to know us very well by now wanted to pass the time of day.

Finally, after leaving the villagers behind we came across the steep path that led up to the cliff top and here we found a flower-strewn hillside where we stopped to gaze in awe at the spectacular scenery surrounding us.

White bellied seagulls soared high above seeming to glide effortlessly against the backdrop of an azure blue sky. While down here on the grass near where we were sitting little grey rabbits played happily scampering here and there totally unafraid; and with the distinct hum of honey bees going about their business and colourful butterflies flitting silently around this indeed was a piece of heaven on earth; and then to top it all I couldn't believe my eyes when the slim body of an exquisite dragonfly the colour of a sapphire hovered gracefully around me and then proceeded to land softly on my shoulder where it remained quite contentedly until something spooked it and it darted away.

I gazed around me in awe at this magical setting noting also the bright pink flowers that bobbed their delicate heads every time a breeze wafted over them; and then I watched entranced as the man ran the flat of his hands gently over the tops of their petals and to my amazement they seemed almost to dance under his tender caress.

I had been in the doldrums on the way up here but the joy on the man's face was infectious and brought to mind these simple words:

The flowers are near
To bring us cheer
Wipe away a tear
Spring is here

I smiled sheepishly to myself, and then, as he broke off a blade of grass and chewed it in a relaxed fashion I was tempted to do the same, but the thought of having to return to London was making it impossible for me to be at ease and my whole body was taut with tension.

So what was I going to do?

Stay here...without him?

That was unthinkable.

Then, before he disappeared from my life completely I needed an answer to a question I had posed a while ago now and so I asked again what He had given us, apart from love that is, which he'd given me in abundance.

Removing the blade of grass from his mouth and frowning he asked, 'don't you know?'

I had to think about that for a bit, and then remembering the scars on his forehead that could only have been made by a crown of thorns, and the livid brown marks on his wrists that had been caused by long spiteful nails that had pinned him to a cross I gazed solemnly at him.

'You gave your life for us...so that we might live.'

Then, as I watched his face tighten with the horror of it all, I was distressed to see tears forming and spill over onto his cheeks, and it was heart-rending to see.

'Don't forget me Mike,' he said.

'I won't...not ever,' I whispered.

And I haven't.

'Well, I don't know about you, but I'm hungry,' and after wiping his face with his sleeve which was such a human thing to do he got to his feet, and leaning over towards me he grabbed my hand and pulled me up to stand beside him.

'Let's you and I go for a last meal together,' and at his words I winced inwardly.

We walked back in silence each with our own thoughts and when we finally approached the cafe in the village we were surprised and pleased to see Maisie and her mother just coming out of the entrance.

They seemed in good spirits and it was great to see them like that, gone were the lines of worry on her mother's face while Maisie herself looked so much better now and she had even put on some weight.

'Well hello,' they called out to us, their faces breaking out into delighted smiles.

Maisie came running up her face aglow with happiness.

'Oh, it's so good to see you again,' and she smiled rapturously first at the man and then at me.

'You look incredible Maisie,' I said joyfully.

Her mother meanwhile seemed slightly perplexed at this outpouring of emotion but then nodding in our direction she smiled and thanked us both profusely.

'Since you came to the house that day this girl of mine is a different person.

Gone is the desire to starve herself, in fact she is eating me out of house and home as you can now see for yourselves. I don't know what occurred that day and Maisie isn't saying but if it was down to you two, then I want to thank you with all my heart as otherwise... I would have lost her,' and with a quick movement she shocked me by leaning forward and kissing me lightly on the cheek; and then she went as if to kiss the man but all at once she appeared overcome with embarrassment and pulled away from him abruptly taking hold of her daughter's arm and saying they must be going now and started walking away back up the hill towards their home while Maisie looked back at us longingly with a silent thank you on her lips.

We decided against having a meal so the man bought a couple of cheese rolls and some hot chocolate and we took them down to the shore and sat on the sea wall.

The tide was well out now and Benny and his friends were on the beach playing a game of cricket.

At some point he saw us and waved cheerily, he also was now totally changed but unfortunately one of his friends who had been with him when they attacked us saw him wave and scowled nastily and spat on the ground in disgust.

'You can't win them all,' I muttered under my breath not realising the man had heard me.

'Maybe one day I will Mike. I live in hope, that's all I can do.'

At this point we could hear the patter of what sounded like tiny footsteps, and then the little figure of Holly arrived before us.

'Hello Jesus,' she exclaimed excitedly hopping from one foot to the other in her excitement at seeing him again.

'I'm terribly sorry,' her mother gushed, rushing up to us and addressing the man. And then she shamefacedly said, 'she has got it into her head that you are Jesus, and even though we have told her time and time again that is impossible she won't be moved.'

'That's ok,' the man smiled gently at her acknowledging her discomfort.

'We have shown her picture books with him in it and...' here she stopped to look at the man curiously and mumbled something that sounded like 'I have to admit though there is a certain resemblance...' and as she turned back to the waiting child who had been standing next to her patiently listening to what she was saying, the questioning look on the woman's face spoke fathoms.

Seeming to pull herself together she quickly announced, 'anyway, we have to go now Holly,' and taking hold of the child's hand she almost had to drag her away.

Eventually, when she couldn't bear it a second longer and freeing herself from her mother's firm grasp she came tearing back to us and placing her two small hands on top of the wall she leant across almost falling into the man's lap and peered intently into his eyes.

'You are him aren't you,' she asked anxiously.
'You are Jesus?'
'Yes, I am.'
'Oh, yes!' and she punched the air with her small fist almost bouncing up and down with delight.
'Holly,' her mother called out in exasperation.
'Come on.'
'Ok,' she called back.
'I'm coming mummy.'

Her face dropped sadly as she murmured, 'bye Jesus,' and off she went dragging her feet after her mother.

'Bye Holly,' and he waved to her just before she disappeared out of sight.

'What a little angel she is,' I said smiling.

'You never said a truer word Mike,' and his eyes twinkled knowingly.

27

The Parting

How do you say goodbye to someone who has become your whole world?

He came to the station with me the following morning straight after breakfast and I was distraught at the thought of being alone again, and especially, I didn't want to leave Him.

He had loved and cared for me when nobody else would. He was my father, brother and best friend and my whole being railed against us having to part.

As we stood side by side on the platform I felt so unbelievably cold, and it had nothing to do with the weather.

'Will I ever see you again?' I asked, choking back tears.

And placing his hands on my shoulders and looking directly at me he answered,

'Yes, but not yet.

Go and live your life my young friend.'

Then as the express train roared into the station my stomach plummeted and steeling myself to walk away I could only manage a few paces before coming to an abrupt halt.

I must have looked pretty miserable for when I swung round for one last look I saw him open his arms to me and he uttered just one word.

'Come.'

Racing back I flung my arms around him and clung on tightly.

I didn't want to let go.

How could I ever let go?

My breathing became shallow, my head reeled and just before everything went black I felt the touch of his beard briefly against my cheek.

28

Returning

I awoke to find myself in a small room with sunshine pouring into it from a large square window.

A uniformed nurse was standing at the foot of my bed peering at a chart that I assumed was mine.

Upon realising I had opened my eyes she smiled sweetly at me.

'Ah, that's good.

You're awake at last.'

'Where am I?

What am I doing here?'

'You're in hospital.'

'I don't understand.

How long have I been here?

What day is it?'

'It's Christmas day.

They brought you in last night with a nasty crack on your head.'

I reached up tentatively and felt a large bandage on my forehead.

'I don't understand,' I repeated.

'I was standing waiting for the train to take me back to London.'

She gave me a quizzical look and shaking her head she then astounded me by saying, 'you were found down by the church and you were lying on the ground with your arms wrapped around the statue of Jesus, they almost had to prise your arms off it.

You were in a bad way, you had hypothermia and would have died if you had been left there much longer'.
Her eyes looked sad as she said,
'You must have been very unhappy.'
'I was going to kill myself.'
'You nearly succeeded.'
I couldn't believe what I was hearing.
They brought me in here, Christmas eve.
'But I've been gone ages with...'
'Who were you with,' she questioned.
'Oh, oh,' I gasped, 'but it can't be.'
Noticing that I was becoming quite agitated she came over to me and took hold of my hand.
'You must have been dreaming.'
'No, no it was so real.'
'Dreams can be like that sometimes, now try not to distress yourself or you will make your headache worse.'
'Worse?
I haven't got a headache.'
'Well you're lucky, you had a great lump on your head and whatever it was you hit it on, it was enough to knock you out.'
I tried to sit up then but she gently pushed me back.
'You just lie there awhile and rest, I'll be back in a bit to see how you're doing,' and with a quick backward glance she left me lying there with all manner of thoughts zipping through my brain.
How could this be?
After a few days bed rest they deemed me physically well enough to be able to leave but mentally I was in turmoil.
Just as I was heading out the door the nurse called me back, and upon reaching into a desk drawer she handed me the roll of money I had found and amazingly it was still tied up tightly in an elastic band.

'I believe this belongs to you although how you came by it judging by how you looked when you were brought in here is anyone's guess,' and she raised her eyebrows expectantly as she waited hopefully for an answer.

But I remained tight-lipped.

'Oh well,' she said sighing, 'look after yourself then young man, and no more thoughts on suicide.'

'Oh, before you go I nearly forgot,' and she reached into the drawer again, 'your glasses were found near where you were lying and luckily they weren't broken.'

'Thanks for all you have done for me,' I said putting on a brave face and I somehow managed to smile gratefully at her, but I had just lost my one true friend and I felt bewildered, confused and very scared.

Putting my glasses on was a revelation as I soon realised that I could see perfectly well without them.

Tears threatened as I recalled the touch of his hands healing me, and maybe also even my eyesight.

Surely it can't all have been a dream; none of it made any sense.

The nurse had given me directions back to the village where they had found me but when I arrived it was all so different.

The cottages and shops were still there but nothing like it was before.

No Cockleshell Inn or Mr. and Mrs. Singh's grocer shop, no Tom or Benny, and no cottage.

I made my way sadly up to the edge of the cliff and gazed out to sea mystified.

My mind must have been playing tricks on me for at one point I thought I glimpsed him standing there holding his jacket out to me, but the next instant he was gone.

The church was still there though and the statue but when I reached out a hand to touch it, it was icy cold and I drew back recalling how warm he had been when I had clung to him terrified.

Had I really dreamt it all due to the bang on my head but then how could I explain my almost perfect vision now - maybe my eyes hadn't been so bad after all.

Reluctantly I decided that I had better head back to London as there was nothing here for me now.

As I waited on the platform for the express to arrive I wished with all my heart that He was there with me and a feeling of absolute sorrow overwhelmed me at the empty place by my side.

29

Never Alone

Arriving back at Paddington after a long and tedious journey I wandered aimlessly about not knowing where to go or what to do. The snow had gone but it was bitterly cold and I was really grateful for the second-hand clothing the hospital had given me.

As I knew I looked reasonably presentable I went into the first cafe I came across and ordered, of course, a hot chocolate; I smiled inwardly recalling how much He had loved it.

My addiction to heroin had now disappeared, my bruises and cuts were all gone and my backside had now healed completely. I couldn't believe how lucky I was except that now there was a large gaping hole in my insides that threatened to tear me apart.

I craved his company.

After leaving the warmth of the cafe I found myself hovering in Covent Garden listening to a busker who was playing a medley of pop songs on a battered old guitar.

He looked as if he hadn't eaten a square meal in days so when he stopped to draw breath, feeling suddenly generous, I rummaged around in my jacket pocket and taking hold of the roll of money I had acquired I threw it into his guitar case, it wasn't mine anyway.

He gazed uncertainly at it with a horrified look on his face and then bending down to retrieve it, he removed a couple of notes, pocketed them, and then handed the rest back to me.

'Thanks mate,' he said, 'but just a couple is enough.'

I was stunned into silence.

'Do you enjoy being a busker that much then?'

'Just another day at the office,' and as he smiled his face lit up and his dark eyes twinkled merrily at me and I was overcome with such wretchedness I had to turn and run away.

'Sorry mate,' he called after me.

'Didn't mean to upset you, but thanks anyway.'

I found a secluded corner and sinking down onto the pavement with my back against a cold wall I gave way to tears and sobbed my heart out.

To say I was bereft would have been a massive understatement.

I just didn't know what I was going to do without him.

I stayed there for what seemed like hours until a little old lady with a walking stick accompanied by a large German Shepherd limped up to me and asked in a soft voice if she could do anything to help me.

She was a dear old thing and I was suddenly ashamed at giving in to such extreme self pity.

'Thank you for asking, but I'm fine now,' and wiping my eyes I tried to smile at her.

'Here,' she said, handing me a bag of hot chestnuts, 'I think you need these more than I do.'

'Oh no, really, I can't take your food,' and I tried to hand them back but she would have none of it.

'Hush now.'

'I was so sorry to see you looking so unhappy, but you know, I think there is someone looking out for you.'

'See here,' and she pointed at something down by my feet.

It was a pigeon squatting there on the floor right next to my foot and not looking for food either as I had none to give.

'I have been sitting on that bench over yonder,' and she stretched out an arm to show me, 'all afternoon watching you and that pigeon hasn't left your side, not once.

Strange don't you think.'

I nodded, strange indeed.

Then reaching down she took hold of my hand and helped me up, and for such an old lady she was really quite strong.

'I have to go now and take my best friend home,' she remarked.

'Oh, I'm sorry to have kept you from them,' I spluttered, looking around me for her companion.

'It's alright dear,' she said, patting my hand gently.

'It's Bruno here,' and she smiled at the huge shaggy bear of a dog.'

'He is my best friend,' and she laughed with some amusement at the look I must have given her.

'I rescued him as a puppy and now we grow old together', and she stroked his big head lovingly.

And then turning her attention back to me she said quite decisively,

'Don't be afraid, for you will never be lonely young man,' and her vivid blue eyes twinkled merrily at me.

And then I knew.

He was with me.

'Goodbye, and take heart,' she said, fondly patting my hand again and even the dog gave me a quick lick; then off she trotted bent over her walking stick and with her best friend padding silently by her side.

To say I was stunned at what had just happened would be putting it mildly.

The pigeon had flown away and the old lady and her dog had gone but I felt uplifted with the knowledge that somehow, in some form or other, He would always be with me.

30

Sam

As I concluded my story I saw that Sam's face was agog with wonder, and also the buzz of conversation that had been there earlier had now fallen silent, and then I saw a couple of women at a nearby table dabbing at their eyes with soggy tissues and I assumed rather uncomfortably that they had been tuning in to what I had been saying.
'Wow!
Was it really Him do you think,' Sam asked.
'Well, whether it was just a case of wishful thinking on my part, fantasy or something more profound I suppose I will probably never know for sure, but what I do know is that the experience changed my life and I'm not the same person I was way back then when I was so broken and lost.
I guess it all boils down to faith and you either believe it or you don't.'
As I now felt quite exhausted I paid the bill and readied to set off home.
'You had better be off to your appointment now Sam, I hope I haven't made you late,' I said, glancing at my watch.
'No, it's fine,' and I was glad to see he appeared quite enthralled by what I had been telling him.
'Thank you for listening and I hope in some way what happened to me will help you.'
'I think it has Sir and thank you for being brave enough to confide in me, it's quite a story.
I only wish He were here now,' he said wistfully hanging his head sadly.
'Not to worry Sam, take heart and believe.'

'I'll try Sir.'

And as we shook hands in farewell I watched as his tense face relaxed with relief.

'Oh sir, your hand is so warm, I can even feel the heat of it travelling up my arm.'

'Maybe that means I have a cold heart,' I said jokingly.

'Oh no Sir, never that,' and he smiled, a real smile for the first time since we met.

'Goodbye Sam, I hope all goes well with you, and I have to say, it's been a real pleasure seeing you again.'

'It's been especially good seeing you too Sir, and I hope to see you again before... well you know.'

'I'm sure you will,' I stated positively.

And as I watched him walk away I was pleased to see that now he had a bit of a spring in his step and actually appeared a little stronger.

I smiled inwardly.

As I made my way home as I had done so many times before I pondered on the events that had happened all those years ago.

I had been in a very dark, lonely place and could see no way out, too much pain for a person to bear, and so my very soul had taken upon itself to take flight and had found comfort in the arms of...Jesus.

His wisdom, strength and tenderness I will treasure forever...but I miss him, and to this day I regret not telling him how much he meant to me, and now it is too late.

And then the tears came.

Epilogue

The End...or a Beginning

When I finally reached home and dried my tears I turned the key in the lock and called out as I always did.
'Hello, I'm home.'
Something smelt delicious and I was glad to at last be indoors out of the chilly weather.
My wife came bustling out of the kitchen with a smudge of flour on her cheek, wiping her hands on her pinny and looking slightly flustered.
'Hello dear,' she said kissing me.
'It's a filthy ol' night.'
'You're right there, have you had a good day,' I asked, eyeing her somewhat tousled appearance.
'Oh you know, the usual - phone keeps ringing and me trying to get the dinner on before you come home.'
'We could always have a takeaway.'
'Oh it's no bother really, I like to cook for you, and besides I'm not keen on takeaway as you already know,' she said, wrinkling her nose in disgust.
'Go and sit yourself down and I'll bring you your sherry, you look a bit pale.
Are you alright?'
'I'm fine, just a bit tired, it's been a long week.'
'You should pack it in now, those kids are wearing you out,' she remarked, helping me off with my jacket.
She went to hang it up but I took it off her and said that I would do it.
'Ok, just as you like,' and she scurried off back to the kitchen.

Placing it up onto the peg by the door I ran my hands gently down the back of it remembering...

As I sat myself down into the old armchair in the small room I had turned into a sort of office I then switched on the gas fire and soon it was warm and snug in there.

I felt so cold.

'Here you are,' and as she placed a glass of sherry on the small table near my elbow she gave me an anxious glance.

'Dinner won't be long,' she said, giving me a worried look with a frown creasing her still pretty face.

'Are you sure you're alright,' she asked, brushing a hand tenderly over my forehead.

I nodded tiredly - it had been such an emotional day.

'Hope you haven't put flour in my hair,' and I gave her a quick wink.

'Oh you!'

Feeling suddenly like a sentimental old fool I took hold of her hand and kissed it.

'I do love you, you know.'

'Yes, I know,' she replied, her eyes smiling happily.

'And I love you too.'

'I'd better finish the dinner - stew and dumplings do you,' she asked sniffing, a bit overcome.

'Just the ticket ol' girl.'

'Not so much of the old thank you,' and off she stalked back to the kitchen kicking a heel up behind her as she went.

As I settled back in the chair at ease now I wondered how Sam was getting on.

Poor boy I thought, he'd had a hard time of it over the years, but he would be alright now I knew with complete certainty.

After a while when the sherry and fire had warmed me I took down a book from the shelf beside me.

When I returned from Cornwall I had been lucky enough to find a place that helped homeless people find somewhere to live and to gain employment.

I had already decided that I wanted to give something back and so I enrolled for evening classes at a nearby college to start getting the qualifications that I would need to become a teacher of religion.

During the day I had been found work in a large department store stacking and loading goods in their busy warehouse.

I was fairly content and if I happened to get any spare time at all I had taken to writing poetry.

I turned to the very first poem I had written which meant so much to me.

Placing my hand over the page I lay my head back and closed my eyes and let it run through my mind.

I knew it so well.

My name is neither here nor there
I wander around almost anywhere
Searching for a place where I can hide
So I will not be espied.
My head is spinning, my bones ache
My empty stomach is starting to quake
I need a fix and I need it quick
Oh God, I feel so sick
I'm a junkie and not proud of the fact
I took the drugs for the courage I lacked
To face life and take it in my stride
You cannot run away and hide
I spend my life searching, for what I do not know
Sometimes I feel so terribly low
Always needing the money to buy
The addictive drugs on which I rely
Passing a church there is a statue outside
A man with such kind eyes I almost cried
He was suffering you could see
But his eyes still loved me
Looking up into his face.
He has oh, such wonderful grace

Dear statue I feel so terribly alone
And you are only made of stone
If only people were just like you
Kind and loving through and through
Maybe then I wouldn't be here
'Clinging to you for all that's dear,' I finished out loud.

A great yearning deep inside me that never went away filled me with such a need I could hardly breathe, and then, with a sigh, I felt my hand slip from the page and fall down lifelessly over the arm of the chair.

******

'Oh hello,' came the excited voice over the telephone.

'Can I speak to Sir please, I have some wonderful news.'

A gasp and then a woman's tearful voice answered, 'no, I'm sorry, you can't speak to my husband. You see... he has passed away.'

Silence from the other end of the line and then a young man's voice catching with emotion replied that he had seen him only a few days ago and he seemed fine then.

'Well, it came as such a shock, one minute he was fine although tired, and the next he was gone.'

And then she asked with a sigh,

'Why did you want to speak to him anyway?

Are you one of his students?'

'Yes, an old one, you see he was always very kind to me and I just wanted to let him know that after having loads of tests the tumour in my head has vanished without trace.'

'Oh, that is good news, and I know my husband would have been so happy for you...as that was the sort of man he was,' she added wistfully.

And then after a long pause...

'There was something odd about his passing though,' she continued with a puzzled note to her voice.

'Oh yes, what was that?'

'I know that some people, when they have died, can look serene and relaxed but...he was actually smiling.'

She heard the sudden intake of breath at the other end of the line, and then...

'I think I could probably enlighten you regarding that.'

www.ingramcontent.com/pod-product-compliance
Ingram Content Group UK Ltd.
Pitfield, Milton Keynes, MK11 3LW, UK
UKHW022215121224
452397UK00009B/197